From Cooperation
to Competition

CHANGE, CHOICE, AND
CONFLICT IN THE
CONGREGATION

Lyle E. Schaller

From Cooperation
to Competition

ABINGDON PRESS • NASHVILLE

FROM COOPERATION TO COMPETITION
CHANGE, CHOICE, AND CONFLICT IN THE CONGREGATION

Copyright © 2006 by Abingdon Press

This book is printed on acid-free paper.

Library of Congress Cataloging-in-Publication Data

Schaller, Lyle E.
From cooperation to competition : change, choice, and conflict in the congregation / Lyle E. Schaller.
    p. cm.
ISBN 0-687-49749-3 (binding: adhesive, pbk. : alk. paper)
1. Church. I. Title.
BV600.3.S33 2006
253—dc22

                                                                    2006000983

All scripture quotations unless noted otherwise are taken from the *New Revised Standard Version of the Bible*, copyright 1989 by the Division of Christian Education of the National Council of the Churches of Christ in the United States of America. Used by permission. All rights reserved.

Scripture quotations marked "NKJV" are taken from the New King James Version. Copyright © 1982 by Thomas Nelson, Inc. Used by permission. All rights reserved.

06 07 08 09 10 11 12 13 14 15—10 9 8 7 6 5 4 3 2 1

MANUFACTURED IN THE UNITED STATES OF AMERICA

To Beth Babbitt Borst

Contents

Introduction

B ut the natural side effect of change is conflict," reflected
Robert Sloan on January 21, 2005, as he announced his resignation from the office of president of Baylor University. "We
moved quickly and boldly to implement the vision (of a new era
for the university) and found that Baylor is not immune to the dis-
comfort and insecurity generated by change."[1]

The central theme of Dr. Sloan's reflections could be used by
dozens of parish pastors every month as they explain their decision to choose early retirement or to resign. It also could be
used by a public school superintendent or the chief executive
officer of a profit-driven corporation or the chief of police in a
large American city or a denominational executive or a city
manager or the spouse who is explaining to his or her parents
the shock of an impending divorce.

A common consequence of change is conflict!

Rather than focus on whether that conflict can and should be
avoided, a more useful discussion can begin by expanding the
subject from two C-words to four. One common consequence
of change is conflict. A second common consequence is change
frequently alters the range of choices available to people. When
change reduces the range of attractive choices, that may generate feelings of resistance, hostility, alienation, and anger. That is
one reason, whenever feasible, to introduce change by adding to
the range of attractive choices rather than proposing changes
that will reduce the number and variety of choices. Make
change by addition, not by subtraction!

1

A third common consequence is change often increases the level of competition. When the discount stores arrived in the 1960s, that created new competition for the five-and-dime variety stores on Main Street. When Wal-Mart, however, began to sell clothing, shoes, auto supplies, jewelry, prescription drugs, and groceries, that created new competition for several other retailers on Main Street!

Those four C-words also can be arranged in three other sequences. Competition often creates change. Competition also may increase choices as well as feeding the fires of conflict. If we begin the sequence with the word choice, we discover that choice often encourages competition and/or produces changes and/or generates conflict. If we begin with the word conflict, we recognize that it often creates new competition and/or expands the variety of choices and/or motivates new changes.

Where Should We Begin?

This book is organized around those four C-words. Each one merits a full book length treatment. Years ago I wrote a book on change and the role of the individual as the intentional agent of planned change initiated from within an organization.[2] Others have provided useful treatments on a variety of expressions of conflict management. In America we are surrounded by an unprecedented abundance of choices. That subject has no natural boundaries.

This observer, however, is convinced that the level of competition for the time, attention, energy, money, allegiance, and participation of Americans stands at an all-time high. That observation may be biased by the fact that I was born into, reared, and educated in a subculture and in an era when cooperation was the dominant theme of my world. I was born and reared on a Wisconsin dairy farm. Farmers had to cooperate with one another in the 1920s and 1930s in order to survive. The road to economic viability for a Wisconsin dairy farmer was paved with stones, each one of which read COOPERATE! The state legislature had decreed that one of the requirements to teach social studies in a public high school in Wisconsin was

2 INTRODUCTION

the satisfactory completion of a course on cooperatives. I spent eight formative years as one of 27–31 pupils in a one-room, one-teacher country school. One lesson that was taught to every pupil every day was the importance of "getting along" with everyone else including the one adult on the campus who held the power position of teacher.

The Great Depression, World War II, and the creation of the United Nations were among the many other components of the American culture that emphasized the importance of cooperation. The ecumenical movement of the 1950s and the 1960s plus the arrival of Pope John XXIII created a new era of cooperation on the religious scene in America during the third quarter of the twentieth century. The flood of denominational mergers in American Protestantism in the 1930–70 era represented another institutional expression of the desire for cooperation in twentieth-century American Protestantism.[3]

Those two paragraphs are included to help explain the choice of competition as the dominant C-word in this book. The shift in agriculture from a labor industry intensive to a capital intensive industry, the suburbanization of the American population during the second half of the twentieth century, the deregulation by the federal government of the transportation industry and financial markets, the economic and political pressures behind the free trade movement, the creation of hundreds of new enclosed shopping malls in the 1960s and 1970s, free agency for professional baseball players, the arrival of retail trade over the Internet, the repeal of the military draft in 1973, and the emergence of scores of nondenominational megachurches were among the expressions of increased competition in the American marketplace.

One interesting consequence of this shift from cooperation to competition came in higher education. Over a period of three centuries religious bodies in the United States had organized and funded the creation of hundreds of colleges, universities, and theological seminaries. One expression of this cooperative relationship was thousands of Christian parents sent their children to a school affiliated with their religion.

Another was denominational agencies, both regional and national, as well as individual congregations, collected and sent money to help fund the budget of these church-related educational institutions. That cooperative relationship peaked in the 1960s. By the 1970s the competition for that growing quantity of charitable dollars had encouraged most of these church-related institutions of higher education to create and staff a development office. As the years rolled by, the creativity and competence of the staff of these development offices enabled them to be able to compete in this new game. By the 1980s the competence of these development offices to build and maintain the relationships with potential donors that served as the foundation for the pursuit of these charitable gifts exceeded the competence of the denominational agencies to compete in this new game.[4]

One consequence was the need to redefine the terminology and the responsibilities of those playing the game. The old rule books of the 1950s and earlier called for those church-related institutions receiving financial subsidies from their denomination to explain and defend their need for continued financial support. This process placed the burden of proof for the continuation of that financial subsidy on the people asking for it to be continued.

As the years rolled by, the people who originally had initiated the request for those financial subsidies and the people who had approved the continuation of those grants gradually disappeared. Their successors relied on precedents. Eventually what had begun as a subsidy evolved into an annual entitlement. When a subsidy becomes an entitlement, the burden of proof shifts. Those advocating a termination of the subsidy are now required to explain why that annual financial grant can and should be terminated. The burden of proof in that process of determining priorities for the reallocation of scarce resources has shifted from the recipient to the donor!

The earlier priority was to subsidize the creation of the new. The new priority is to subsidize the perpetuation of the old. This expression of the competition for financial aid currently

4 INTRODUCTION

can be seen in the production of a variety of goods and services including cotton, both air and surface transportation, higher education, nuclear power, housing, health care, the planting of new missions and the resourcing of congregations, ministerial placement, and the funding of a variety of religious organizations.

One consequence of this change is thousands of institutions founded by Christian religious bodies in the United States are now able to compete more effectively for charitable gifts than are the religious bodies that funded their creation. A second has been the termination of the relationships between what is now a well-financed institution of higher education and the religious body that created it.

In 1701, for example, Congregational ministers in New England founded Yale College to prepare men to serve as Congregational ministers.[5] In 1757 a worshiping community was organized at Yale that eventually became known as the Church of Christ in Yale. The building housing what was Yale Chapel was occupied in 1876. A series of twentieth-century mergers produced the successor denomination, the United Church of Christ, to the Congregational Church. In 2004 a university committee recommended one way " . . . to strengthen the growing expressions of religious and spiritual life" at Yale would be to discontinue the affiliation of the chapel congregation with the United Church of Christ. The recommended date to terminate the relationship was July 2005.[6] One consequence was a wave of discontent among dozens of adults who had become long tenured participants in the life of that chapel community.

Those who use a longer time frame for reflecting on change may recall that Harvard College, founded in 1636 by the Puritans and largely controlled by Congregational ministers, experienced a termination of that relationship with the Congregationalists two centuries earlier in 1805.[7] As goes Harvard, so goes Yale?

Change often generates competition for the loyalty of individuals. Competition often creates conflict. Conflict frequently motivates people to seek new choices for their participation.

From Cooperation to Competition

That short paragraph introduces the first of two central themes of this book. The American religious scene of the 1910–70 era was marked by a growing degree of intercongregational, interdenominational, and interfaith cooperation. The anti-Catholic sentiment that was a powerful divisive force in American Christianity as recently as the 1950s disappeared as the result of several million funerals. The civil rights movement of the 1960s generated unprecedented coalitions of Catholics, Protestants, and Jews. The Vatican opened the doors in the 1960s to unprecedented warm relationships between Catholics and Protestants.

The 1960s also saw the arrival of an unprecedented level of competition in the secular economy in America. The Germans and the Japanese became serious competitors in the design, manufacture, and sale of motor vehicles. Railroad passenger service could not compete with air travel and the convenience of that network of interstate highways. Merchants on Main Street could not compete with retailers in the new shopping centers. The availability of convenient offstreet parking became a decisive factor in the competition for customers among retailers, medical clinics, motion picture theaters, churches, restaurants, travel agencies, and banks.

Competition Undermines Retention

The erosion of inherited institutional loyalties fed the growth of the free market. One expression of this was Presbyterians found it easier than their parents to switch from a Presbyterian congregation to an Episcopal or Methodist church. For many the most surprising facet of this new free market in the American religious landscape was the number of persons born and reared in a Roman Catholic family who switched their religious affiliation to a Protestant church began to approach and eventually exceeded the number switching from Protestant to Catholic. The BIG surprise, however, was the millions of Protestant churchgoers who found it easy to switch from an inherited affiliation with a denominationally affiliated Protestant congregation to a new nondenominational Protestant church. One factor, of course, was the invitation to "Come and help pioneer the new" often has more appeal than "Come and help us perpetuate the old." As Methodists, Lutherans, Presbyterians, and others cut back sharply on organizing new congregations, the resulting vacuum in the ecclesiastical free market was filled by others.[8]

One measurable indicator of this erosion of denominational loyalty is in the database of what today is The United Methodist Church. In 1956 the 39,845 congregations in the Methodist Church reported receiving a combined total of 309,760 new members by letter of transfer from other Methodist churches. The Evangelical and United Brethren congregations reported nearly 10,000 new members received by intradenominational letters of transfer. For 1980 the 38,417 congregations in The United Methodist Church reported a combined total of 171,926 members received by intradenominational letters of transfer. For 2002 that number of intradenominational transfers of membership for the 35,102 United Methodist congregations was down to 109,069, slightly more than one-third the number back in 1956.

One interpretation of those numbers is they represent a natural and predictable consequence of a more competitive religious marketplace. Another interpretation is the American churchgoers born in the 1890–1940 era displayed a far higher degree of denominational loyalty than do the adults born after 1940. A third is a substantial majority of United Methodist congregations today are too small to be able to mobilize the resources required to produce the quality, relevance, and choices younger generations expect. A fourth is if that retention rate had dropped by only one-half since 1956, this would be a numerically growing denomination.

A fifth is the population in the United States increased by 74 percent between 1956 and 2002. If the number of congregations had increased by 74 percent from slightly over 44,200 congregations in the two predecessor denominations in 1956 to

77,000 in 2002, that would have provided twice as many intradenominational options for the Methodist seeking a new church home in 2002 than were actually available. (In 1906 the six predecessor denominations reported a combined total of 57,087 congregations or one church for every 1,500 residents of the United States. A total of 77,000 congregations in 2002 would have averaged out to one church for every 3,750 residents.) To produce that net increase of 33,000 in the number of congregations probably would have required planting at least 50,000 new missions between 1956 and 2002. That would have required a high priority on evangelism and missions year after year and could have produced a denomination that by the end of 2002 would have reported a combined average weekend worship attendance of 8–10 million, considerably higher than the reported total of 3.5 million for 2002.

One response to this challenge to retain the allegiance of members is to explain it as a natural and predictable consequence of competition. General Motors, United Airlines, grocery stores, pharmacies, and department stores have been experiencing the same problem. The Service Industry Research Systems, Inc. reported in 2005 that back in 1982 department stores accounted for 70 percent of the retail sales of men's apparel, 75 percent of women's apparel, and 64 percent of children's clothing. By 2004 those proportions had dropped to 38 percent, 35 percent, and 36 percent respectively. In 2004 department stores accounted for 4 percent of the retail sales of home furnishings and electronic items, down from 25 percent in 1982! Retail sales of furniture plunged from 40 percent in 1982 to only 3 percent in 2004.[9]

Sam Walton, Southwest Airlines, Toyota, free trade, specialty stores, and the "big boxes" have made the American economy far more competitive today than it was twenty-five years ago!

A different response, however, often is heard in congregational circles. "We joined this congregation back in 1965 when Reverend Adams was the pastor. Our worship attendance was over 600 back in the 1960s. Ever since he left, it has been dropping. Last year it was down to under 400. What we need is another pastor like Reverend Adams."

A more realistic appraisal might resemble this statement. "We joined this congregation back in 1965 when Reverend Adams was the pastor. He was an expert on timing. He came here when this church enjoyed little competition for the loyalty of members. The real competition among the churches in this community for future constituents did not begin until 1974 when the first of what are now three nondenominational megachurches was organized. Adams had the good sense to accept a call to another church with little real competition and left here in 1972. Today our congregation is competing with at least a half dozen other larger churches that have new facilities with plenty of offstreet parking at far better locations than we have. I am grateful our current pastor has been able to avoid a greater decline in attendance!"

The New Religious Revival

Weekend worship attendance in American Protestant congregations sets new records year after year. One tiny part of the explanation is the migration of "Cradle Catholics" to Protestant congregations. From a larger perspective one big reason for that 50 percent increase in Protestant worship attendance between 1965 and 2005 was the increase in the population. A second was the arrival of what has been described as the fourth great religious revival in American history.

Several religious bodies plus thousands of entrepreneurial individuals saw this as an opportunity to expand their evangelistic outreach. One example is the Evangelical Church of the Covenant. In the thirteen years from 1991 through 2004 the combined average worship attendance of their affiliated congregations increased by 64 percent. One part of the explanation is one-fifth of their congregations serve an ethnic minority constituency. Another factor is an unusually large proportion of large congregations—7 percent—reported an average worship attendance of more than 500 in 2004, more than double the proportion for all of American Protestantism.

The big new and highly visible player in this post–1960 game of proclaiming the gospel of Jesus Christ to Americans, of course, is represented by the hundreds of nondenominational megachurches averaging more than a thousand at weekend worship. Another consists of thousands of new congregations created to reach and serve recent immigrants from the Pacific Rim, Latin America, India, Mexico, and Africa. A third, and even larger in the total impact, consists of American religious bodies including the Southern Baptist Convention, the Assemblies of God, the Baptist General Conference, the Evangelical Free Church in America, the Seventh-day Adventists, the Churches of Christ, and scores of other movements, associations, conferences, conventions, and denominations. Sam Walton and his colleagues invented a new way to do retail trade with younger generations. These religious bodies have been inventing new ways to do church in an exceptionally competitive ecclesiastical marketplace.

What Happened?

"We went back in our records for the reporting year ending in 1954 through 1958 inclusive," explained one denominational official. "We found that over those five years slightly more than one-half of our congregations reported an increase in their membership. We followed the same methodology for the period January 1, 2000 through December 31, 2004. Over those five years we found only 32 percent of our congregations reported an increase in their membership. When we deleted the churches that had disappeared via dissolution, withdrawal, or merger into another congregation or reporting exactly the same membership at the end of 2004 as they reported at the beginning of 2000, the percentage reporting an increase climbed to 36 percent, but that is far below 50 percent. How would you explain that pattern?"

"First of all, I have not studied the trends in your denomination," replied the seminary professor to whom this question was addressed. "Therefore I can only speculate. I have analyzed the membership trends in several other mainline Protestant denominations in America plus five smaller denominations. On the basis of that research I can speculate and suggest a dozen factors that might help to explain what happened. You, however, will have to choose the ones you believe are relevant to your denomination and rank them in order of influence. I have had enough firsthand experiences with congregations in your denomination to enable me to guess about three or four of the half dozen most influential."

"What's your number one?" challenged this denominational official. "My guess is you'll tell us we don't have an adequate number of pastors who are driven by a passion to evangelize the unchurched."

"No, that's not my number one. In fact, if I build a list of the ten most influential factors, that would rank about number sixteen."

"You've got to be kidding!" exclaimed one of the other four denominational officers in the group. "I could see why you might place that third or fourth but sixteenth! Why?"

"The answer is I place a strong reliance on systems theory to help me understand the world I live in today," explained Professor Anderson. "I am not arguing that you do not have a shortage of parish pastors who have a passion for evangelism. That may be true. My question is why has your system produced that shortage? Rather than scapegoat individuals, I prefer to begin by asking why that system produces the outcomes it is producing. That emphasis on a systems approach has led me to conclude that the number-one factor in explaining the numerical decline of congregations is the frequency of a serious mismatch between what that congregation needs at this point in its history and what the current pastor brings in terms of gifts, skills, personality, passion, priorities, experience, potential tenure, marital status, leadership style, and theological stance."

"Why do you include marital status in that assortment of variables?" interrupted another of the denominational officials.

"My experiences have convinced me that effective parish pastors are happy pastors," came the reply. "If that pastor is married, that often includes being married to a spouse who is happy being married to a parish pastor, who is happy to be living in that particular community and who also is happy being married to the minister of that particular congregation. If you pushed me on that variable, I probably would move it up to the first or second variable. In my travels I've seen too many congregations in which the unhappy spouse produced a brief and relatively ineffective ministry in that parish.

"To return to the point I was attempting to make," continued Professor Anderson, "I am convinced the differences among people in general and among the clergy in general are far greater today than they were in the 1950s. In addition, the differences among congregations may be even more pronounced today than they were fifty years ago. Let me give you a simple example. That new pastor arrives and is driven by a passion to evangelize the unchurched. The congregation, however, is divided with strong support for each of five different priorities. One-fifth want the new minister to recreate the good old days of 1980. One-fifth see the top priority to be rebuilding the Sunday school. One-fifth want a loving shepherd who will spend an hour every week with each of three or four dozen elderly members who live alone or are in nursing homes. Another 20 percent are convinced the youth of today represent the church of tomorrow and want the new minister to build and nurture a big ministry with teenagers. The remaining 20 percent are convinced that the way to attract young families is with outstanding preaching that is the heart of a presentation-type worship service designed around a pipe organ, a robed choir, classical hymns, and a preacher in a pulpit."

"I've been there many times," affirmed one of the denominational officials. "I hear what you're saying. That good match between pastor and congregation is the number-one variable."

"That introduces my second variable," continued Professor Anderson, "and this also reflects a big difference between today and the 1950s. In the 1950s a less than ideal match between pastor and congregation was not as disruptive as today. One reason is in the 1950s life in America was still organized around functions and respect for authority. Today a far greater value is placed on relationships. Fifty years ago a sick person went to a doctor who diagnosed the problem and prescribed a remedy.

Today the quality of the interpersonal relationships between physician and patient is recognized as a powerful factor.

"In addition, back in the 1950s the member who became discontented with the new pastor tended to leave rather than organize an internal quarrel. The decrease in respect for persons in positions of authority makes it easier for a handful of discontented members to organize and succeed in ousting the current pastor. Change often does generate divisive internal conflict that leads to premature resignations.

"Today we recognize the value and influence of long-term relationships. Therefore, if your database includes the necessary information, I suggest you review the trends you described earlier. My hunch is you will discover that the congregations in which the typical pastorate was two to seven years were more likely to experience numerical decline than was the pattern in those in which the typical pastorate was at least a decade in length."

"If I understand correctly what you're suggesting," came another interruption, "these two factors overlap. Good matches tend to produce long pastorates, and long pastorates are a key to continued numerical growth."

"That's the point," affirmed Professor Anderson. "Those two go together, and my research suggests both are more influential today than they were fifty years ago.[10]

"The most important point you raised in comparing the historical record of the 1950s in your denominations with a more recent era suggests that fifty years ago more than half of your congregations appeared to be effective in reaching, attracting, serving, assimilating, nurturing, and challenging the generations of Protestant churchgoers in America who had been born in that 1880–1940 era. The vast majority of those folks have died. The challenge today is to reach adults born after 1950. That is a far more difficult assignment!" explained Professor Anderson.

"One indicator I use in identifying the Protestant congregations in America that are most effective in attracting and serving younger generations is how long they have been gathering at the same address for the corporate worship of God. The work I've done in Latin America and Africa suggests that the majority of the rapidly growing congregations have been meeting at the same address for fewer than fifteen years. In the United States a more useful number is forty years, but some will argue it is closer to twenty-five years. After a quarter century at the same address the natural institutional tendency is to focus on taking better care of the current constituency and their children, not on evangelism. In other words," summarized the professor, "if more than one-half of your congregations have been meeting in the same building at the same address since before the mid-1960s, you probably are a numerically shrinking religious body."

"Are you suggesting we should plant more new missions?" questioned one of the officials.

"That is part of the strategy," came a quick agreement, "but the driving generalization is the future-oriented churches are more likely to be sensitive and responsive to the expectations and needs of younger generations than are the churches driven by local traditions from the past. Invite younger generations to help pioneer the new. Don't expect them to be eager to come and help perpetuate the past! One indicator I suggested earlier is to determine the percentage of congregations that have been meeting at the same address for more than forty years. Frequently the relocation of an existing church's meeting place can be the equivalent of a new mission. A second indicator is the death rate of your members. If the annual death rate of your confirmed members is above 12 per 1,000 confirmed members and rising, that suggests an inability to attract younger generations. In 2004 the death rate in America was 10.7 per 1,000 residents age 14 and over."

"Three of us have to leave now to catch our plane," apologized one of the denominational officials. "You have given us a lot to think about, and we would like to hear more, but can you summarize your central theme for us before we leave?"

"I'll try," replied Professor Anderson. "We began this conversation with your comparison of the proportion of congregations in your denomination that reported an increase in membership in the 2001–2004 period compared with the proportion back in the 1954–58 era. That survey provided some useful data for your diagnostic processes. As you design a ministry strategy, I would offer four suggestions. First, instead of relying on membership data to measure change, a more useful indicator may be average worship attendance. Congregations vary greatly in their definitions of that word membership. Some have a high threshold into membership while others have a low threshold. Adults born after 1950 are less likely to seek formal membership in any organization including lodges, veterans' organizations, religious congregations, or political parties than were their parents and grandparents.

"Second, you may find it more helpful to develop a set of criteria that can be used to identify the congregations that are competitive. I believe that will be more helpful than simply focusing on numerical growth. For example, the congregation that increases its membership, or its average worship attendance, from 18 to 27 over the space of four or five years will be reported as experiencing a 50 percent growth rate, but it is not competitive. What may have happened is two or three families moved into the community and joined that church. In most large suburban communities a Protestant congregation probably needs to average at least 350 at worship to be competitive in reaching adults born after 1960. I live in a large suburban city in which fifteen of the seventy-four Protestant congregations average 700 or more at worship. Fourteen of the fifteen either were organized after 1965 and/or have relocated their meeting place at least once since 1975.

"Over the years several surveys have reported that approximately one-third of all Protestant congregations in the United States were experiencing a decline in membership, one-third were on a plateau in size, and one-third were reporting numerical growth. A more recent survey of Southern Baptist congregations added a category called "healthy" and reported only 11 percent could qualify as healthy churches.[11] While I would use different criteria, my guess is that fewer than 15 percent of all the Protestant congregations in America can be described as competitive. One simple operational definition of that term looks at the families that moved to town and began to shop for a new church home. These are committed Christians who are taking the initiative to find a church. Over a period of a few months each one worships with a dozen different congregations. How many return for a second visit before making a final choice? Typically no more than two or three. If you prefer a statistical criterion, how many congregations receive a number of new members for three consecutive years that is equivalent to at least 10 percent per year?

"My third comment before you leave is, if you are designing strategies that congregations on a plateau in size or that have been experiencing a long-term decline in worship attendance can adopt and customize to fit their local situation, you need to ask the question, 'What if it works?' If that congregation does become competitive and begins to attract and assimilate significant numbers of newcomers, one price tag usually is more changes than many of the old-timers can tolerate. A related price tag is change usually generates conflict. A third is the strategy to become competitive in the effort to attract and serve younger generations of churchgoers usually requires increasing the range of choices in music, in worship, in learning opportunities, in personal involvement in doing ministry, in building a personal social network, and in participation in meaningful and memorable experiences that nurture the personal spiritual journey of the individual.

"Finally, the historical record is clear, given the choice between making the changes required to become competitive or gradually fading into obsolescence, the majority of individuals, voluntary associations, religious congregations, profit-driven corporations, and nonprofit institutions find it easier to adjust to obsolescence rather than initiate and implement the required changes."

The Either-Or Question

This extended conversation with Professor Anderson introduces the second theme of this book. Normal human beings

INTRODUCTION

naturally tend to be reluctant to make either-or decisions. We prefer the both-and option. Should I eat a bowl of ice cream while watching the late evening news on television? Or should I attempt to reduce my weight? Normal Americans answer, "Yes!" to both questions.

Congregational leaders ask, "How can our congregations compete for the allegiance of younger generations of Americans without making disruptive changes in our ministry?"

Denominational leaders ask a parallel question, "What can we add to our strategy to increase the proportion of our congregations that will be competitive in reaching, attracting, serving, assimilating, nurturing, challenging, and transforming the lives of Americans born after 1965?"

Both questions evoke the same response. That is not a useful way to state the issue. For most American organizations and institutions providing person-centered services, the real issue can be summarized in two questions.

The first is there are only two roads leading into the future for your institution. Which one will you choose? The more heavily traveled one in American Protestantism is the road to obsolescence. One reason it may attract such heavy traffic is there are only a few widely separated tollbooths.

The second road into the future begins with a big sign reading, "The road to becoming competitive. This is a road marked by tollbooths every few miles. Are you willing to pay the tolls required to travel down this road? The most frequent tolls include a willingness to change, creative responses to disruptive internal conflict, and expanding the range and variety of choices offered people. This is a long road and is marked by scores of tollbooths. You will have to pay each of these tolls more than once if you want to continue your journey."

The first tollbooth on this particular road requires reading a chapter designed to help you understand how the bar for acceptable performance has been raised all across the American economy. The second tollbooth asks for an explanation of how the rule book for your church has been revised. The third stop is not a tollbooth. It is a rest stop for those who want to sit, relax, make a few calls on the cell phone, and marvel at the recent rapid pace of technological change. The fourth toll requires reading a long chapter that identifies several of the consequences of this rising level of competition. The fifth toll-booth in this book is where we add a fifth C-word to our collection. Here we reflect on an ancient guideline. We count what we believe to be important and what we count becomes important. The focus is on what you should count to help you choose the important criteria in defining such categories as "healthy" or "competitive" or "relevant."

At the sixth stop we explain why it is important for you to continue to drive in the right lane on this road into tomorrow. When life is marked by large quantities of discontinuity with the past, we need the reassurance of continuity and hope. One sign of hope is what we call "light at the end of the tunnel." One expression of continuity is what Alvin Toffler has described as a "stability zone."

At the seventh stop the discussion shifts to looking at the safety valves that can reduce the pressure created by internal conflict.

At a longer eighth stop on this road we double the number of C-words. The sixth C-word is categories. How can we understand the growing complexity of life that is one of the tolls for traveling the road to becoming more competitive? We need relevant categories to divide that complexity into small components of contemporary reality that we can comprehend and communicate to others. (For those who are counting, we are now up to twelve C-words: competition, change, conflict, choices, count, continuity, categories, complexity, components, contemporary, comprehend, and communicate. For those who want to enlarge that list, we can add three more C-words. This traveler's observations suggest a common characteristic of those congregations that have been attracting a disproportionately large number of churchgoers born after 1965. They proclaim, "What we teach, what we believe, and what we do" with remarkable clarity, a high degree of internal consistency, a strong emphasis on certainty, and an absence of ambiguity.)

At the next-to-last stop on this road we pause to reflect on a few of the implications and consequences that go with that important C-word "choice."

Finally, since gambling is now a way to raise money for many good causes such as education, public transportation, and health care, we offer an optional stop where you are invited to choose the probable winners in this competition among religious organizations in America to attract younger generations of churchgoers. An optional side trip at the end of this toll road is included for those who want to check the references for the numbers scattered through the text.

The second of these questions assumes you have decided to pay the tolls and make the changes required to be competitive in the twenty-first century. Who has both the authority and the responsibility to initiate those changes? That question requires a customized response by each congregation and each denominational agency. In each case well-informed insiders need to be engaged in that process.

CHAPTER ONE

The Bar Has Been Raised!

I n the Olympic contests of 1900 a Frenchman won the marathon race in a time of 2 hours, 59 minutes, and 45 seconds. One hundred years later in the summer Olympics of 2000 a Japanese athlete won the marathon in 2 hours, 10 minutes, and 11 seconds. The Olympics opened the door for women to run the marathon in 1984. The first woman to cross the finish line that year, Joan Benoit, finished in 2 hours, 24 minutes, and 52 seconds, more than a half hour less time than the male winner in 1900. The bar had been raised!

● ● ●

In April 2005 the retail price on a pair of jeans varied greatly. At Wal-Mart the prices ranged from $10 to $25. In other stores, a pair of True Religion jeans was priced at $359 compared to $325 for a pair of Levi's Premium while a pair of Evisu's limited edition jeans for men cost $635.[1]

● ● ●

By 1983 it had become apparent that this thirty-five-year-old congregation had outgrown its site. The three building lots purchased in the middle of a residential subdivision were considered adequate back in 1948. As the congregation grew in numbers, a dozen nearby houses were purchased and removed. That land was required for additional construction and for parking. Eventually the decision was made to relocate the meeting place. Two adjacent parcels of land at an excellent location were on the market. One was sixteen acres. The other was fifteen acres. Which should they buy? The wise decision was made to purchase both. The congregation did relocate and continued to grow. Twenty years later it was obvious they should have continued their search until they had found a site covering at least sixty acres at an attractive location.

● ● ●

Those who enjoy reading congregational histories can find scores of examples of Protestant congregations in America that averaged fewer than forty at Sunday morning worship in the early 1930s, but were able to enjoy the services of a full-time resident pastor. Today an average worship attendance of 110–135 is seen as the minimum for a congregation seeking to attract and retain the services of a full-time minister who is a seminary graduate. That means at least two-thirds of the Protestant congregations in the United States are not able to compete in the ministerial marketplace. That bar also has been raised. One option is for the pastor's employed spouse to subsidize the arrangement with a good paying job that also provides employer-paid family health insurance. Another is a series of short pastorates by students or retired ministers. A third is for one pastor to serve two or three small churches concurrently.

● ● ●

In 1987 the largest congregation in The United Methodist Church reported an average worship attendance of 3,235, and a total of three reported an average worship attendance of 2,500 or more. Fifteen years later the largest congregation in that denomination reported an average worship attendance of 7,100, and seventeen congregations reported an average worship attendance of 2,500 or more. By contrast, a total of eighteen Southern Baptist congregations reported a worship attendance of 5,000 or more on the last Sunday in 2003, and seven reported it was between 7,000 and 18,500. The bar has been raised on the definition of the "very large church"!

The Erosion of Inherited Loyalty

Fifty years ago Christian congregations and denominational systems in the United States enjoyed loyalty from the constituents that often was inherited from earlier generations. For many church members that inherited institutional loyalty was reinforced by ancestry. Religious bodies in America frequently were identified by two words such as Irish Catholic, Swedish Baptist, German Methodist, Norwegian Lutheran, Dutch Reformed, Polish Catholic, German Evangelical, Italian Methodist, Swedish Covenant, German Lutheran, and Scotch Presbyterian.[2] That loyalty also often was reinforced by marriage vows. A common practice was the wife transferred her allegiance to her husband's religious ties, but husbands also made the switch.

One way to reinforce denominational loyalty was for Lutheran parents to send their son or daughter to a Lutheran college. That increased the probability that one consequence would be a Lutheran-Lutheran marriage. Presbyterians, Catholics, Methodists, and other parents also supported denominational colleges for the same reason. That larger religious system was designed to reinforce institutional loyalty. It worked.

Today religious bodies in America have to compete for the loyalty of younger generations. Instead of being inherited, that loyalty has to be earned and re-earned. Interdenominational and interfaith marriages are far more common. One common consequence today is when the Roman Catholic marries a Baptist, the couple agrees on a three-point treaty. We will not join a Baptist congregation. We will not choose a Catholic parish. We will choose a religious affiliation that is new to both of us. Egalitarianism requires creating the new rather than perpetuating the old.

As recently as the 1950s and 1960s American churchgoers who were changing their place of residence often placed a high value on geographical proximity in choosing a new church home. While a decreasing number walked to church, neighborhood ties reinforced a member's loyalty to a particular denominationally affiliated church. During the past few decades the large regional church has replaced the small neighborhood congregation.

One consequence is Christian congregations are competing with other Christian congregations for future constituents. Denominations are competing with other denominations, and with nondenominational independent churches for future constituents. A variety of surveys, polls, and studies indicate that in the mid-1950s only 5 percent of American churchgoers had switched to a different religious affiliation from the one in which they had been associated as a child. Three decades later that proportion had climbed to more than 30 percent. By 2005 it was closer to 40 percent. Competition makes retention more difficult!

One denominational response is to choose not to compete and watch the constituency grow older in age and fewer in numbers.

The suburbanization of the population, the lengthening of the journey to work, the two wage-earners couple, the two-car garage, and the erosion of inherited denominational loyalties created a market for the large regional church. One consequence was an increase in competition for future constituents. The neighborhood congregation that drew most of its worshipers from within a three-mile radius of the meeting place served an area of approximately 28 square miles. The regional church serving people living within seven miles of the meeting place identified an area covering approximately 154 square miles as its parish. That redefinition of the parish area from a three- to a seven-miles radius could increase the number of competing congregations sixfold!

That, however, understates what happened. The 1920–70 era represented the peak of an era in American Protestantism that was marked by such concepts and practices as ecumenism, interdenominational cooperation, denominational mergers, comity, and Christian unity. It is unreasonable to expect anyone born after 1960 to fully comprehend the power of that movement for greater cooperation among American Christians since they did not experience it.[3] One consequence of that movement for greater cooperation and more denominational mergers was to erode the loyalty to both congregations and to denominational systems that was such a valuable asset in the 1950s.

The Impact of Death

Overlapping that was another factor called death. The Christian churchgoers in America who were born in the 1860–1940 era tended to display a high degree of loyalty to their religious system. Most attempted to transmit that to their children. In addition, those generations also tended to respect persons in positions of authority including pastors, professors, presidents, physicians, and bishops. As a group they tended to be comfortable with organizational structures designed with a top-down system of governance.

The generations of Americans born after 1940, as a group, tend to prefer governance systems built on horizontal partnerships. They are comfortable challenging the statements and expectations issued by persons in positions of authority, they expect institutions to earn and re-earn the allegiance of their constituents, they find it relatively easy to switch their church allegiance across the old lines of demarcation, and, if discontented, they find it easy to quietly depart. This has created problems for the American manufacturers of motor vehicles, for department stores, for the commercial airlines, mainline Protestant denominations, colleges, and universities competing for the best and brightest of this year's high school seniors, for professional sports teams, and for at least seven out of ten Protestant congregations in the United States

To make it even more threatening, all of the contemporary evidence suggests the generations born after 1960 will outlive those born before 1940. Those congregations and denominations seeking to replicate their ministries of 1955 probably can retain the loyalty of more churchgoers born before 1930, but that is a shrinking constituency!

The Impact of Technology

Technological changes have transformed the American culture during the twentieth century. One example is the combination of national radio networks, motion pictures, and television has sharply reduced the influence of accents in oral communication. The forty-year-old born and reared in Massachusetts and the forty-year-old born and reared in South Georgia, unlike their grandparents, find it relatively easy to understand what the other is saying. That does not mean they will agree with one another on the best candidate for the office of President of the United States or on a variety of divisive *pelvic issues*, but the road to agreement begins with good communication.

One of the two big technological changes that has increased the level of competition among the churches for future constituents was described earlier. That is the relatively low price of the privately owned gasoline powered motor vehicle. When a good used car could be purchased for the equivalent of two months' income or less, that fed the growth of the large regional church.

That also created a new line of demarcation between congregations that could be defined as competitive in the quest for future constituents and those that are not competitive. A widely used guideline begins with the question, "What is your total worship attendance on a typical Sunday morning in May or October?" In 1965 the advice was, "Divide that number by four, and that is how many offstreet parking spaces your congregation should own." If a congregation averaged 140 at the early service and 220 at the second, that formula (140 + 220 divided by 4) suggested 90 parking spaces was sufficient to be competitive. Today the number 2 has replaced the 4 in that formula. If that same congregation now averages 80 at the early service, 160 at 9:30 a.m., and 200 at 10:45 a.m., the new formula (80 + 160 + 200 divided by 2 = 220) suggests a need for more than twice as much parking, even though worship attendance increased by less than one-fourth. The bar has been raised.

The combination of television and videotapes also has raised the bar on what people should be able to expect from church in terms of quality, relevance, and choices. Back in the 1950s the churchgoers born in the 1880–1940 era tended to rely on four reference points as they articulated their expectations of a congregation. One was the congregation in which they had been reared. A second was the congregation to which they had belonged before moving to their current place of residence. A third was "the church down the street." The fourth was the church where they worshiped while visiting relatives or friends on vacation.

What Are the New Reference Points?

Today the churchgoers born after 1950 are more likely to use a different set of reference points as they formulate their expectations of the church. One may be a worship service they watched on television. A second may be the conversations at work or with a neighbor on the ministry of a megachurch that person attends. A third reference could be a "tourist stop" visit to a two- or three-day event sponsored by a large teaching church.

A fourth may be a worship experience, while visiting friend or relative, in a congregation in which the message is delivered, not by a live person in the room, but by projected visual imagery on a screen. That messenger usually ranks among the top 2 percent of all preachers in contemporary American Protestantism in communication skills. Any minor glitches have been eliminated in the editing of that videotape or DVD. The content of that message probably would rank among the top 10 percent of the sermons preached in America on that weekend in quality and relevance.

Back in these churchgoers' home congregations their pastors may rank among the top 45 percent in both delivery and content (nearly all of today's parish pastors in American Protestantism were born and reared in Lake Wobegon, Minnesota, and therefore are above average), but that is not as competitive as being among the top 10 percent. Technology has raised the bar.

Can American Protestant congregations be evaluated in terms of their effectiveness in reaching, attracting, serving, assimilating, challenging, discipling, and equipping for ministry in today's world the generations of Americans born after 1960?

One response is that is an heretical question! Worshiping communities are called by God to be faithful and obedient. Those are the only two legitimate criteria for evaluating their ministry.

A second response comes in the form of a question. If most of the 325,000 Protestant congregations are competitive in reaching the unchurched population, why have an estimated 30,000 missionaries and pastors come to America from Asia, Africa, Latin America, and Europe to evangelize the unchurched?

A third response also is stated as a question. If these 325,000 or more Protestant congregations are competitive, why are there so many self-identified Christian believers in America who do not have an active and continuing relationship with any worshiping community? The number of adults in that category is approximately equal to the number of believers who do have an active and continuing relationship with a community of Christian believers. In a few denominations the number of confirmed members is double the average worship attendance. Does that suggest the threshold into confirmed membership is relatively low? Or that the threshold at the exit is relatively high? Or that these self-identified Christian believers are waiting to be challenged rather than simply counted? Or is that one way to persuade these believers to move to the sidelines? Or that they believe in God the Creator and Jesus the Savior, but not in the church?

The Denominational Dilemma

It could be argued that the number-one victim of the increased level of competition for the allegiance of younger generations of Americans has been the larger religious bodies such as the Roman Catholic Church in America, The United Methodist Church, the Presbyterian Church (USA), the Evangelical Lutheran Church in America, the Episcopal Church USA, the Lutheran Church–Missouri Synod, the American Baptist Churches in the USA, the United Church of Christ, the Christian Church (Disciples of Christ), the Reformed Church in America, and, more recently, the Southern Baptist Convention.

They, and their predecessor denominations, filled a clearly defined role in the 1950s, but their future is now threatened by at least a dozen trends and forces. The most obvious of these factors was discussed earlier. Tens of millions of the loyal supporters of 1955 have died. Their replacements bring questions and challenges, not inherited loyalty and obedience. Systems designed by and for adults born in the 1860–1940 era often are perceived to be obsolete, irrelevant, or counterproductive by younger generations. That generalization applies to veterans' organizations, tax-supported public high schools,[4] political parties, alumni associations, lodges, county agricultural fairs, labor unions for adults employed in the private sector of the American economy, neighborhood churches, transcontinental passenger trains, sheds on the church grounds in the North to shelter the horses while the owners were in Sunday school and worship, the family-owned and operated hardware on Main Street, and large denominational systems filled with anonymity and complexity.

One consequence is described by the polite term disengagement. The adult churchgoers of 1955 had been reared in a culture that emphasized the values of loyalty and obedience. World War II reinforced those values. Those values undergirded the obligation to "Pray, pay, and obey." Those American religious systems that traced their history back to Rome or to the Church of England inherited that in their DNA.

For the past four decades, however, the American culture has taught younger generations another option. "If you're discontented, walk away." That was one reason for terminating the military draft back on June 30, 1973. One expression of that is the large number of Americans born and reared in a Catholic or Lutheran or Methodist or Presbyterian family who have found it easy to switch their religious affiliation to another Protestant tradition or to an independent church.

A second expression of disengagement is that growing number of Protestant congregations that have terminated or switched their denominational affiliation. That trend surfaced first in what today is the United Church of Christ, the Christian

Church (Disciples of Christ), the two large Presbyterian denominations, and the Lutheran Church–Missouri Synod. More recently that virus of disengagement has spread to the Evangelical Lutheran Church in America, the Episcopal Church USA, the Southern Baptist Convention, and The United Methodist Church.

Another expression of disengagement is the reduction in the proportion of congregational financial income that is forwarded to the regional judicatory and/or national denominational agencies. In the 1960s that percentage often was in the 10–20 percent range. Today it is more likely to be in the 3–10 percent range. Hundreds of denominationally affiliated congregations averaging more than a thousand at worship forward less than 3 percent of their total financial receipts to denominational headquarters.[5]

One explanation is that several denominations organized and funded a variety of church-related institutions (colleges, hospitals, theological schools, camps, homes, et al.) that have created a system for soliciting gifts of charitable dollars that is more effective than the system operated by the parent denomination.

A fourth facet of disengagement that can be defined as either cause or effect comes in the form of ideological or theological statements. The parishioners say to the denomination, "If that is the road you're choosing, we're taking a different path into the twenty-first century." That expression of disengagement has been heard frequently in Lutheran, Episcopal, Presbyterian, Roman Catholic, Southern Baptist, United Methodist, and Christian Reformed circles.

Who Resources Congregations?

Fifty years ago Protestant denominations in America earned and re-earned the loyalty of members by resourcing congregations. The denomination created, produced, and distributed resources for the Sunday school. The denomination published hymnals back before projectors and screens replaced the hymnal racks on the back of pews. The denomination assisted in ministerial placement. The denomination designed, staffed, and administered conferences and workshops for congregational leaders. The denomination provided experienced and expert help in conducting capital funds campaigns. The denomination owned and operated camps and retreat centers. Denominationally affiliated theological schools were created and financed for the education of the next generation of parish pastors. The denomination was the basic building block in interdenominational cooperation. The denomination recruited, trained, equipped, placed, and supported missionaries to evangelize the unchurched on other continents. The denomination organized and funded new expressions of ministries. The denomination planted new missions.

During the past half century a variety of competitors have been created to resource congregations and to do what denominations formerly did. These include a growing variety of parachurch organizations, retreat centers, interdenominational agencies, councils of churches, tax-supported state universities, individual entrepreneurs, church-related institutions of higher education, teaching churches, and specialized single function organizations.

The big new kid on the block is the megachurch, averaging 3,000 or more at worship, that sends missionaries to a dozen different countries, produces resources on how to do church in the twenty-first century, and creates new expressions of ministry.

A reasonable estimate is one-half of all churches under that broad umbrella called American Protestantism have made taking care of their members and transmitting the Christian faith to the next generation two of their top four priorities. (The other two often are taking care of their real estate and paying their bills on time.) Another 49 percent (maybe only 30 percent?) have made congregation-building one of their two or three top priorities.

The remaining 1 percent have combined kingdom-building and creating new expressions of ministry as their top two priorities.

One of the unintended consequences is these kingdom-building churches gradually have been replacing denominational systems as the number-one source of help on how to do church in this new millennium. It is not a coincidence, for example, that the most influential book (*The Purpose-Driven Life*) for lay study groups, (a) was written by the founding pastor, Rick Warren, of a relatively new megachurch rather than by a denominational official or a seminary teacher, (b) was published by an independent firm, not a denominational publishing house, (c) focuses on the personal faith journey of the individual, rather than on how to reinforce denominational loyalties, and (d) has been introduced into their congregations by Lutheran, Presbyterian, Methodist, Catholic, and other pastors.

In summary, one consequence of this increase in the competition to resource congregations has been an expansion of the attractive choices available to congregational leaders. A second consequence has been the introduction of new models for congregational life that are not built on the foundation of a denominational affiliation. A third has been a huge increase in the role and influence of the laity. A fourth has been the inevitable conflict between denominational priorities and practices and those advocated by this new wave of competitors. (The dirty word for this consequence is "congregationalism.") A fifth is what was described earlier as disengagement. A sixth has been an increase in the level of competition for the charitable contributions of individuals and the discretionary dollars in congregational treasuries. A seventh is the high value placed on interdenominational and intercongregational cooperation in the 1920–60 era has been replaced by a goal to find the road to relevance and viability. An eighth is many denominational systems, at both the regional and national levels, are being confronted with two choices—change to become competitive or continue to drift down the road to obsolescence.

The National Context

While these could be described as natural and predictable consequences of an increase in competition, the plight of the

FROM COOPERATION TO COMPETITION

larger religious bodies in America has been undermined by four other changes on the national scene.

The most highly visible has been the change in the sources of immigration into the United States. Those religious bodies that traced their origins back to Western Europe found it relatively easy to reach and serve immigrants from Germany, Scandinavia, the Netherlands, Italy, and Great Britain. It has been more difficult for them to assimilate recent newcomers from the Pacific Rim, India, Latin America, the Caribbean, and Africa.

A second change came with the greater demand for transparency and accountability in large and complex institutions. That long list includes trading on the nation's stock exchanges, the performance of tax-supported public schools, the delivery of health care, the stewardship of resources in large profit-driven and investor-owned corporations, journalism, and governmental agencies. In recent years one of the most highly visible examples of this demand for public accountability came with the pedophilia scandals involving hundreds of Roman Catholic priests, thousands of victims, and hundreds of millions of dollars in awards to the plaintiffs. A Catholic layman, Jason Berry, began to report on this problem in 1984, but denial silenced the public press for nearly two decades.

That incident illustrates how the combination of the absence of a system of internal accountability reinforced by denial can generate conflict, undermine confidence in that institution, and encourage disengagement. The bar has been raised on the definition of acceptable accountability for institutional behavior!

A third change has been the American culture is less supportive of organized religion today than it was in the 1950s or even the 1980s. The emergence of unbelief in the United States as a viable and defensible position for mature adults has been traced back to the middle third of the nineteenth century.[6] During the past quarter century atheists and agnostics have redefined unbelief as the superior worldview. One expression of that stance is a change in the language of self-identification. The self-identified "Brights" now explain, "I don't believe in the tooth fairy, I don't believe in Santa Claus, I don't believe in the Easter bunny, and I don't believe in God."

Unbelief is a more serious competitor for the allegiance of Americans today than at any time since 1607. While unbelievers have more adherents in several European countries than in the United States, it clearly is more widespread and acceptable here than it was in 1955 or 1985. While not widely discussed, the rise of unbelief has changed the cultural context for denominations in the United States.

The fourth change, like disengagement, appears to be contagious. This is an increase in polarization. The highly visible expression of polarization is in partisan politics at both the national and state levels of government. Polarization over conflicting ideologies also can be seen on the campus of scores of universities, in how to pay for health care, how to fund Social Security, over the best design for motor vehicles, within the movement to conserve the environment, in how to reduce boredom in the public high schools, and on acceptance of the death penalty. One reason well over 99 percent of the readers of this book were relieved when they were not asked to succeed Pope John Paul II was they did not want to face the polarization among Roman Catholics in America on their long list of highly divisive issues.

One expression of the polarization in several large Protestant denominations in America is over control. Who will control the policy-making processes in your denomination? Your caucus? Or some other interest group?[7]

A persuasive argument can be made that in several of the larger denominations in American Protestantism a five-stage process begins with the polarization of the constituency over ideological and theological issues. That leads to conflict over control. The third stage is marked by the disengagement of many of the constituents. The natural and predictable fourth stage is to move institutional survival and/or the care of the clergy to the top of the denominational agenda. When that replaces missions, evangelism, and the resourcing of congregations at the top of the denominational agenda, the final stage is institutional and functional obsolescence.

Does your denomination fit into that five-stage scenario? Who has both the authority and responsibility to answer that question? If it does fit, what stage is your denomination in today? Who has both the authority and responsibility to answer that question? If the constituency is polarized over several divisive issues (four of the most common over the past twenty centuries have been *pelvic issues*, doctrine, polity, and control), who has both authority and the responsibility to resolve this internal conflict in the first stage or two before disengagement becomes the most common response?

Internal conflict, polarization, and the battle over control are three of the most common consequences of an increase in the level of competition. That sentence helps to explain why the bar for relevance and viability has been raised in several religious bodies in the United States in recent decades.

One consequence is fewer resources are available for interchurch cooperation. A second consequence is that an increasing number of congregations and denominational systems are now faced with the choice between change and continuing to drift down the road to obsolescence. A third is the call to be an effective parish pastor is a far more difficult assignment today than it was in the 1950s. A fourth consequence is the rule books are being rewritten all across the American landscape including for the institutional expression of the Christian faith.

CHAPTER TWO

What Do the New Rule Books Say?

T he shock of 9/11 revised the priorities for the United States Congress in allocating money.

The demands on state legislatures and local governments to appropriate more money for education, pensions, the delivery of health care, public safety, and transportation have forced them to raise taxes or to seek new sources of revenue. One consequence has been to rewrite that rule book. The new rule book includes a greater reliance on grants from the federal government, on "sin taxes" (gambling, tobacco, alcoholic beverages), on direct receipts from state-sponsored gambling, such as lotteries, and on consumption taxes and fees for services.

The shift from defined benefits to contribution-based pension plans has revolutionized how Americans plan for their retirement. The termination of the military draft on June 30, 1973, has transformed the system and the costs for building military forces in the United States. Television has revised the rule book for public speakers from oratory to conversational messages wrapped in entertainment. Medicare and Medicaid have produced radical revisions in the rule books for those delivering health care services.

The combination of state legislation in the middle of the twentieth century to encourage the consolidation of public elementary and secondary school districts plus the more recent enactment by the federal government of the No Child Left

Behind legislation has almost completely obliterated the assumption that the design, administration, and funding of tax-supported public education is the responsibility of the adults who live within a short distance of those school buildings.

During the nineteenth century private transportation was facilitated by the construction of toll roads and canals charging user fees. In the twentieth century that rule book was rewritten to provide tax-supported roads and highways. During the past six decades it has been revised again to increase the number of toll roads.

The change from the open outcry system of buying and selling stocks and commodities on this nation's exchanges to electronic trading has produced a new rule book and eliminated a lot of jobs. Global competition has produced a new rule book for the manufacture and export of motor vehicles. In early 2005 the hourly compensation rates for workers in the motor vehicle industry were $49.60 in Germany, $40.96 in Japan, $36.55 in the United States, $5.87 in Brazil, and $1.96 in China.

The old rule book for Protestant congregations in America declared that a rapid increase in population in the community created opportunities for an increase in membership. The new rule book explains that a rapid increase in population usually generates greater competition among the churches. A common consequence is many of the congregations that have been meeting at the same address since before 1965 shrink in numbers while the new missions that are designed to be competitive in the twenty-first century grow in size.

The old rule books called for congregations in rural America to cooperate with one another in order to survive. The new rule book calls for congregations in rural America to expand their service area in order to compete for future constituents.

The vast majority of the 2.95 million babies born in the United States in 1920 grew up in a home without a telephone. Their formative years were spent in a culture that taught them the four primary channels for communication were (1) facial expressions and body language, (2) the spoken word, (3) the handwritten or printed word, and (4) pictures including still photographs.

The vast majority of the 4.16 million babies born in the United States seventy years later in 1990 own a cell phone. Their formative years have been spent in a culture that has taught them the four primary channels for communication are (1) facial expressions and body language, (2) the spoken word, (3) moving visual images projected on a screen, and (4) music.

The old rule book in American Protestantism called for proclaiming the Good News about Jesus Christ by the spoken word, the printed word, and music. The new rule book calls for proclaiming the Good News by projected visual imagery, music, and the transformation of people's lives.

In the 1950s theological seminaries and divinity schools were expected to equip students with the skills required to be a scholarly teacher, a persuasive preacher, a creative administrator, an effective evangelist, a popular youth leader, an empathetic pastoral counselor, a visionary leader, a respected representative of that church in the larger community, and an enthusiastic supporter of that denomination.

That not only prepared the graduate to be the pastor of a congregation, but also to plant a new mission, to revitalize a dying church, to serve as a denominational official, or to serve on interchurch committees.

By the 1970s the rule book for the practice of law, the practice of medicine, the practice of teaching, and for leadership roles in a variety of organizations had been transformed. In order to compete in the new American economy, specialists were groomed to replace generalists. This new model did not expect one person to possess all the gifts, skills, wisdom, and experience required to excel in all facets of the assignment. The small public high school with a half dozen teachers, one of whom also served as the principal and another doubled as the athletic coach, was replaced by the large consolidated school with a team of specialists.

Teams began to replace the solo performer. Instead of sending one minister out to plant a mission designed to plateau with an average worship attendance of 125 at the end of five years, the new rule book called for sending a team to staff a model designed to produce a new congregation averaging at least 600 in worship at the end of three years. Instead of staffing the large congregations with a collection of individuals, the new rule book calls for a staff composed of a team of teams. Where is the best place to learn how to be a member of one of these teams? In seminary? Or by serving on one of these teams in a very large church where the new rule books are being produced?

Back in the 1950s denominational leaders followed a rule book that focused on how to increase the membership by organizing new missions, by encouraging central city congregations to relocate to suburban communities, by greater interdenominational cooperation, and by the merger of denominations. In the 1960s the Church Growth Movement produced a series of new rule books that explained how existing congregations can attract new constituents. In the 1970s new rule books were written on how to increase the influence and role of intradenominational caucuses, interest groups, and lobbies. One consequence was an increase in the level of intradenominational quarreling.

By the 1980s the new rule books were being written by that growing number of nondenominational megachurches with the top priority on the transformation of people's lives. One consequence was leaders from denominationally affiliated congregations began to study these rule books, rather than rely on denominational resources, as they planned for the future of their congregation in the twenty-first century.

During the late 1990s leaders in several denominations concentrated on producing new rule books that would encourage congregations to send more money to finance denominational budgets.

The rule books of the 1970s and 1980s evaluated dentists on the basis of who could craft the best dentures. Today dentists frequently are evaluated on the basis of who excels in cosmetics or who can create the whitest teeth and the brightest smile?

First-time visitors to a Protestant congregation in 1955 may have evaluated that congregation on the quality of the chancel choir or the sermon. Today the criterion may be the contagious enthusiasm of that ten- or fifteen-person worship team or on the range of choices offered for the corporate worship of God every weekend. In some denominations today one criterion for the evaluation of congregations is how many dollars have been forwarded to denominational headquarters, but rarely is that among the criteria used by those first-time visitors. They are more likely to ask, "Did this worship experience speak to me on where I am on my own personal faith journey?"

Tens of thousands of Protestant congregations all across America are still relying on a rule book, or a ministry plan, designed in the 1950s to reach and serve Americans born before 1935. That may not be the appropriate manual to use in designing a ministry plan to reach and serve Americans born after 1960. Among the many differences in that 1956 edition and the 2006 version are these. Committees have been replaced by ministry teams. Sunday morning worship may be led by a worship team rather than a robed chancel choir. In Christian education the old focus on teaching has been replaced by a greater emphasis on learning. The teacher-led adult Sunday school class has been replaced by peer-driven learning communities. The new position of ministry of missions has been filled by a person, often a laywoman, who challenges lay volunteers to spend seven to fifteen days as short-term missionaries working in ministry with fellow Christians in a sister church on another continent. The old rule book placed a high priority on "creaming off" the best of the lay volunteers for assignments in administration. The new rule book challenges the cream of the volunteers to be engaged in doing ministry.

The old rule book called for the minister to deliver the sermon while standing in or behind the pulpit. The new rule book urges the preacher to walk around while delivering the message.[1] The new rule book also states the sermon may be delivered in person by the resident pastor or via videotape by a total stranger who combines superb content with a high level of competence in oral communication.

The old rule book called for organizing a youth group that included four grades of high school students. That was consistent with the educational scene of the pre–World War era when the vast majority of youth attending high school were enrolled in schools with a total enrollment under 350 and the culture offered teenagers two choices—take it or leave it. The new rule book suggests organizing teenagers around points of commonality other than age, grade, or gender—similar to the central organizing principles used in the very large public high schools today. The new rule book affirms replacing the pipe organ with a band or orchestra. Instead of sending money to denominational headquarters to help fund a new mission, the congregation may choose to accept and fulfill the role of a multisite church. Instead of looking to the denominational headquarters for resources, the congregation is more likely to purchase these from a parachurch organization. Instead of defining the primary constituency by their place of residence and their denominational affiliation, the new rule book is more likely to define the primary constituency by where they are on their own personal faith journey or by their theological stance or by their personal social network or by their ancestry or by their ideological position on social, economic, and political issues or by their hopes for their children or by some other variable that cannot be described by their geographical proximity to that congregation's meeting place.

The dress code for Sunday morning worship has been relaxed from "Sunday best" to "casual." The threshold into membership has been raised so the average worship attendance often exceeds the number of voting members. The staff person who specialized in children's ministries has been replaced by a person who specializes in ministries with families that include children. Instead of asking two or three small congregations to share the same pastor, the new rule book urges small congregations to affiliate with a large missionary church.[2] Instead of building on weakness, the new goal is to combine weakness with strength. Instead of constructing one very large room so the entire congregation can worship God together in the same room at the same time, the new rule book urges providing two or three venues for worship and scheduling three or four or five or six or seven DIFFERENT worship experiences every weekend. Instead of looking for full-time ordained generalists, the new staff configuration may call for more part-time lay specialists.

Six Questions

1. Has the day arrived when the local or the denominational rule book that defines the system of governance, the priorities in the allocation of scarce resources (including the time and energy of volunteers), the traditions that must be perpetuated, the public image of that congregation, the typical tenure of pastors, and the specialties in ministry must be revised for your congregation to be competitive in the search for future constituents?
2. If yes, who has both the authority and the responsibility to initiate that revision?
3. Does your current rule book focus on the obligations members are expected to fulfill in order to be described as faithful members of this congregation? Or is your rule book organized around the theme of the transformation of believers into fully devoted disciples of Jesus Christ?
4. The old rule book often focused on congregation-building, on strengthening the life, ministry, and vitality of that congregation. The new rule book is more likely to focus on kingdom-building, on strengthening, and on expanding the kingdom of God. Which is the primary focus of your congregation's rule book?
5. If your congregation carries a denominational affiliation, is the rule book used by your denominational leaders consistent with and supportive of the theme of your congregation's rule book?
6. When was the last time either rule book was revised around the central theme of reaching, attracting, serving, assimilating, nurturing, challenging, discipling, and equipping for ministry the generations of Americans born after 1960? Or should that responsibility be assigned to the new churches founded since 1985 with their new rule books?

CHAPTER THREE

The Electronic
Swiss Knife

Should I telephone my wife's parents in New York to tell them our baby has arrived and both mother and child are doing fine?" wondered the new father in Chicago as he left the hospital. By the time he reached home, he had decided to write a letter. The postage would be three cents. The cost of a three-minute daytime station-to-station telephone call from Chicago to New York was $2.20. The year was 1937. The average hourly wage for a production worker in manufacturing was $.62. An additional motivation not to make that call was his home did not have a telephone. He would have had to impose on a neighbor to make the call. In the United States there were only 15 telephones for each 100 residents in 1937.

●　　●　　●

Thirty-five years later in 1972, the Federal Communications Commission was considering granting permission to AT&T to create a new wireless network for telephone service. That motivated the Motorola Corporation to begin research on manufacturing wireless cellular phones. The Motorola Dyna 86600X hit the retail market twelve years later. It weighed two and one-half pounds and cost $3,995 plus tax. After allowing for inflation, that would be the equivalent of nearly $8,000 in 2006.

●　　●　　●

It was the eighth inning of the seventh game of the American League Championship Series in major league baseball. The winner of this series would represent the American League in the World Series. The date was October 19, 2004. The Yankees had a runner on first base. The third baseman for the New York Yankees, Alex Rodriguez, hit a bouncing ball in the infield. The pitcher for the Boston Red Sox, Bronson Arroyo, fielded the ball and tagged Rodriguez for what appeared to be the second out of the inning. Rodriguez, however, with his left hand slapped the ball out of Arroyo's glove. As the ball rolled away, Derek Jeter, the Yankee shortstop who had been on first, crossed home plate. Rodriguez, who represented the tying run in what had become a 4 to 2 game, stopped at second.

Play was stopped as the six umpires met to discuss the correct way to call the play. Fans in the stands were confused. No announcement was made over the public address system. A replay was not shown on the electronic scoreboard since major league baseball forbids showing disputed plays. Rodriguez was declared out, and Jeter was sent back to first base. The run did not count.

How could the fans in the stands, most of whom had paid a substantial amount of money for a ticket to the game, understand what had happened?

For those who came prepared to utilize modern technology, the solution was easy and convenient. Pull out that cell phone and dial a friend or relative who was watching the game on television. Request an explanation of what had happened.

● ● ●

Six months later, in mid-April 2005, the 115 cardinals of the Roman Catholic Church met to elect a successor to Pope John Paul II. They met in the Sistine Chapel in Rome. One of the many measures taken to guarantee secrecy was the installation of a device under the raised floor in the chapel that would jam all incoming and outgoing cellular phone calls.

● ● ●

By that time the combined number of land line telephones and cell phones in the United States exceeded the number of residents. The big users of cell phones, on a per capita basis, were countries such as Taiwan, Finland, South Korea, the Czech Republic, and Norway.

●　　●　　●

What are the memories that are celebrated when a tragic incident takes the life of a teenager? Her smile? Her friendly spirit? Her church relationship? Her affection for a sibling, parent, or cousin? Her achievements in school? Her love for young children?

When a seventeen-year-old girl was found dead of what was suspected of being a drug overdose in December 2004, the mourners celebrated her life by lifting up the 17 things she loved so dearly. They included her grandfather, roses, a rap musician, shopping, and her cell phone.

●　　●　　●

Alexander Graham Bell secured the basic patent for transmitting human speech over a wire in 1876. The capability to transmit the human voice from Point A to Point B hundreds, and eventually thousands, of miles away represented discontinuity with the past. It was a vast improvement over talking, yelling, sending messages on paper or in code (smoke signals, flag waving, the telegraph), or with drawings and photographs. The automatic switchboard for telephone calls and the portability of the cordless telephone could be described as evolutionary changes.

Sending the human voice from Point A to Point B without a connecting wire (radio) also could be described as simply another evolutionary change.

For most of the twentieth century telephone service was classified as a public utility. It was regulated by the government. It also was the recipient of subsidies derived from taxation. In 2003, for example, $3.3 billion was collected and paid out in subsidies to help finance rural telephone service. The deregulation of the telephone industry of the 1980s ended an era of protection from serious competition.

Four Themes

The central theme of this book is change generates competition which expands the range of choices available to people. That produces greater competition which creates new changes which enhances competition which creates additional choices. That becomes a self-perpetuating cycle. A common side effect of that cycle is the generation of disruptive conflict.

A secondary theme is technology produces changes that generate new choices and greater competition. Will the cell phone or the iPod be the successor to the Sony Walkman? The growing demand for the multimedia cell phone and the growing demand for multimedia worship experiences are parallel trends in the early years of the twenty-first century.

A third theme is younger generations of consumers bring far greater expectations to the marketplace than did their parents and grandparents. Many of those expectations evolve into demands that produce both new choices as well as greater competition and more changes.

In broad general terms the deregulation of the telecommunication industry and the recent rapid rise in the level of competition illustrate all three themes. .

A fourth theme, which is really a consequence of those first three themes and was lifted up in the previous chapter, is the past three or four decades have brought an unprecedented era of discontinuity to many facets of American life. Telecommunications represents one example of discontinuity. A second is in American foreign policy. A third is in the role of religious organizations in creating and administering social services. Back in the 1960s liberal Democrats strongly supported a greater role for the churches in housing the elderly, in community organization, in the nation's war on poverty, in building and administering housing for low income families, and in urban renewal. Four decades later many liberals opposed the use of tax funds for faith-based initiatives.

A fourth example of discontinuity is in the delivery of health care with reliance on a third party payer. A fifth is in the use of the Internet to finance political campaigns. A sixth is in retail trade. A seventh is in the economic and demographic reversal of the decline of the central business district in scores of American cities.

An eighth is the numerical decline of several mainline Protestant denominations that were able to compete for the allegiance of churchgoers born in the 1880–1940 era but have been unable to compete effectively for the loyalty of many of the sons and daughters of those older generations. A ninth is how interchurch competition has replaced the interdenominational cooperation of the 1950s and 1960s.

An interesting symbol of this discontinuity is the cell phone. That is the primary explanation for this brief side trip down memory lane. The first commercial cellular telephone call originating in the United States was made in October 1983. By the end of 1985 the American economy included slightly over 340,000 cell phone users. Two decades later that number had jumped to 165 million! Never before had a new invention gained such rapid acceptance.

Back in December 1965 a station-to-station, daytime, 3-minute telephone call between New York City and Denver cost $1.70. After allowing for inflation, that would be approximately $10 in 2006 dollars. In the early 1990s a 3-minute cell phone call from New York to Denver cost a couple of dollars. Today the cost is so low few cell phone users stop to calculate it. In December 2004 a woman in New York City was shopping for a new iPod mini for her nephew in Australia. She was surprised to discover it came in several colors. Which color should she choose? She whipped out her cell phone, called her sister in Australia, and told the clerk, "I want it in blue."

The increase in competition after the 1996 decision to open up more of the wireless spectrum was a significant change. One consequence was in 2003 cell phone conversations came to a total of 830 billion minutes according to the Cellular Telecommunications & Internet Association. That was about 74 times the volume twelve years earlier in 1991! The number of international telephone calls between the United States and another nation increased more than sixfold in only seven years from 984 million in 1995 to 5,926 million in 2002!

Expanding Choices

The reason for choosing the cell phone as a symbol of discontinuity was *not* to discuss the options available to Clark Kent when the time comes to change clothes. One reason is the cell phone does illustrate the rapid pace of technology-driven change. Technology-driven change often increases the degree of competition. The telecommunications industry is one example of that effect. Since the deregulation of the telephone industry in 1984, the impact of technology-driven change has accelerated, and that has raised the level of competition.

Another reason is to illustrate that fork-in-the-road created by competition—adapt or become obsolete. The arrival of the cell phone has forced the traditional telephone companies to make difficult changes in a hurry. A big third reason is the addition of a camera to the cell phone supports the contention that human beings naturally tend to prefer to communicate by visual imagery rather than the spoken word. This is a revolutionary discovery for those responsible for planning an experience designed for the corporate worship of an invisible God.

One reason for this side trip is the cell phone illustrates how technology can enable institutions to skip a stage rather than follow a slow evolutionary sequence. How can telephone service be made available to poor people in the third world? One response is the expensive process of digging holes in the ground, putting up a series of tall poles, and stringing a network of wires. The current alternative is the wireless cell phone. That same issue is being resolved in the same way all across rural America. The old answer was tax-funded financial subsidies. The new answer is the wireless phone.

A parallel question on the American religious scene is how long will it take a rural Protestant congregation, organized in 1871 to serve the residents of this village founded as the marketplace for a farming community constituency, to adapt to a new context for ministry? Thirty years ago those farms began to be transformed into residential subdivisions, retail shopping centers, medical clinics, entertainment opportunities, and parking lots. The number of residents of this larger community

FROM COOPERATION TO COMPETITION

increased from 3,800 in 1950 to 115,000 in 2000. The average worship attendance at this church has increased from 85 in 1950 to 115 in 1975 to 140 in 2005. That looks good when compared to the congregation meeting in a building three blocks away that was founded in 1853. Their average attendance had climbed from 63 in 1950 to 110 in 2005. Nine of the ten largest Protestant congregations currently serving this community either (a) were founded in 1980 or later and/or (b) have relocated their meeting place since 1980.

The veteran leaders of these two congregations keep asking, "Why do the people moving out here prefer one of those megachurches over our congregation?" The most frequent realistic response sounds rude but can be summarized in five words. "Your congregation is not competitive."

A more useful explanation begins with the question, What do people do in church? In both of those congregations mentioned here, the answer is not much different today than it was in 1950. We gather to worship God, to pray, to sing, to listen to a sermon on God's word, to share in the Sacrament of Holy Communion, and to volunteer in the Sunday school and youth program as a part of our effort to transmit the Christian faith to our children. We socialize with old friends and kinfolk. We celebrate weddings and baptisms; occasionally we welcome new members. We gather to mourn the death of a friend or relative. We come together to bid farewell to a departing pastor or to welcome a new minister. We collect money and send it away to hire people to do ministry on our behalf. Some of us meet in weekly Bible study and prayer groups. We plan and staff a vacation Bible school every summer. We attract a big crowd every December 24 to our Christmas Eve service. We eat together several times a year. Several of us serve on committees and boards. We pay a minister to serve as our pastor. We maintain this building that was constructed back before any of today's members were born, and we conduct one big fundraising event every year to help balance our budget.

What do people do with cell phones? A lot more than they did with a landline telephone in 1986! Instead of being a wireless version of the telephone on the desk, the cell phone has become the electronic Swiss knife of this new century. People talk while they walk or shop or drive or wait in line or watch television or eat or work in the yard. They pay for that ride in a taxi with their cell phone. They may have cut their charge card into small pieces because their new cell phone also serves as a charge card. While serving on another continent, they stay in touch with the folks back home. They download music or check their glucose level with their cell phone. They take and transmit digital photographs with their cell phone. They plug into the Internet on their cell phone. They play poker online. For about $12 to $15 a month they subscribe to a service that transmits cartoon movies to a cell phone as a way to entertain their two-year-old child while traveling. They watch major league baseball games on that tiny screen. They use their cell phone to scan documents and transmit the data to a computer. A growing number terminate their landline connection and rely completely on a wireless telephone connection. Teenagers use their cell phone to call close friends—and sometimes their parents—several times a day simply to "stay in touch." By relying on a portable cellular phone, they have reduced the availability of coin-operated telephones in airports and other public places. The husband searching the aisles in the supermarket calls his wife for advice on how to shop. Others use their cell phone to check their bank account or to thumb text a message to a friend or to make an investment in stocks or to learn how their favorite sports team is doing or to purchase a new ring tone or while watching a TV program.

The cell phone has replaced the radio as the number-one training resource for those mastering the art of multitasking.

Parents pay the extra $15 a month for a service that uses satellites to trace the location of a cell phone, the speed it may be traveling, and the direction it is going and reports these data to the designated Web site.

The cell phone has become a security device for people out alone after dark. It is a source of instant gratification. One version of the cell phone comes with a body-mass-indicator and a target-rate-calculator for those engaged in a fitness routine. It also may include the weekly schedule of exercises such as an hour on the stair climber on Monday, the list of barbell exercises for Tuesday, and the elliptical trainer for Wednesday. Instead of recruiting a few hundred people for a protest demonstration against a governmental policy or decision, the cell phone makes it easy to enlist thousands.

Competition creates choices, and choices produce winners and losers. One of the losers is the hotel that made a profit on in-room telephone service. That average annual profit was well over $600 per room in 2000, but dropped to $150 by 2004. How can pollsters interview what is a representative cross section of the American population? In 1995 calls to landline telephones provided an acceptably accurate close cross section. The increase in cell phone users who do not rent a landline telephone has undermined the validity of that sample.

The combination of affluence plus the 85 percent decrease in the per-minute cost between 1996 and 2006 in the use of a cell phone has both increased the number and variety of services and its use. The arrival of the third generation of cell phones in 2004 symbolized the rapid rate of change in the contemporary world.

What Does It Symbolize?

The cell phone is not simply one more innovation in an evolutionary process for transmitting the human voice from Point A to Point B. The cell phone represents radical change and substantial discontinuity with the past. The person traveling from New York to Los Angeles in 1950 may have made the trip by train. The thirty-year-old grandchild is more likely to make that trip by air. The commercial air carrier represents radical change and substantial discontinuity with the past. The family who made a reasonably comfortable living on an 80-acre farm in 1936 now has a grandson who farms 800 or 2,800 acres. The discontinuity is from a labor intensive operation to a capital intensive business.

The cell phone symbolizes the recent rapid acceleration in the pace of change. In the 1940s a small number of new parents took black-and-white movies of that new baby. The next five decades brought the super 8mm silent movie camera for amateurs, the sound-on-film movie camera, and the VHS camcorder. More recently the tiny 8mm movie camera, the digital camcorder, and the cell phone have expanded the range of choices.

The four-generation evolution from the silent black-on-white film movie camera to the VHS camcorder required fifty years.

The first generation of cell phones was born in the early 1980s.

The second generation arrived in the 1990s.

The third generation, broadband, arrived two decades after the birth of that first generation in late 1983.

A parallel is in the evolution of Sunday morning worship in most congregations in American Protestantism. The era of the traditional presentation-type worship service (except for the spirit-filled congregations) extended through the 1950s. The first generation of nontraditional worship began in the 1960s with the arrival of that first wave of the "new" Christian music. The 1960s also saw television introducing color into what heretofore had been a black-and-white culture in the churches. Maroon robes for the choir was an earlier break with tradition. The 1970s brought the beginnings of what evolved into radical discontinuity with tradition as participatory worship began to spread across the country. The 1980s saw preachers using overhead projectors to provide motionless visual imagery for sermon illustrations. The 1980s also brought another new wave of Christian music, and the 1990s brought a third wave.

The 1990s brought a new generation of technology that, like most departures from tradition, evoked strong opposition. The demand for "contemporary worship" that included a faster pace and the new music was growing. That was matched by a growing demand for high quality and relevant "teaching messages" delivered by an exceptionally competent communicator. The shortage of ministers who could meet those high expectations created a problem.

One response was invented by a handful of creative pioneers in Rockford, Illinois, who organized the nondenominational (or tradition-free) Heartland Community Church in 1998. In July 1999 they celebrated their first anniversary with two firsts. That was the first time in their brief history their attendance had ever exceeded 1,400. It also was the first time the message had ever been delivered in person by a live messenger! By 2005 the congregation had grown to the point where it purchased an enclosed shopping mall as its next meeting place.

The use of projected visual imagery in full color, rather than reliance on a live messenger, for delivering that oral message during the corporate worship of God represents tremendous discontinuity with the past for most congregations. However, it represents continuity with daily life for tens of millions of churchgoers who have been watching the delivery of the network news on evening television ever since Walter Cronkite's era. Several mature adults shrug this off as a recent point of discontinuity with the past as they explain: "This is nothing new! I began to get used to receiving important messages by projected visual imagery back in the 1930s when I watched the newsreels in the neighborhood movie theater."

For tens of thousands of small Protestant congregations this can provide continuity with the past as the people continue to gather with friends and relatives to worship God every Sunday morning in that familiar room filled with sacred memories. They are inspired and challenged by relevant sermons prepared and delivered by excellent communicators of the gospel of Jesus Christ via projected visual images. The opposition to change, the conflict generated by change, and the pressures of competition have produced an interesting response. When confronted with three choices, (1) sharing a full-time loving shepherd who is a second-rate preacher with another congregation or (2) disbanding or (3) combining the part-time paid services of a trained lay pastor with superb preaching delivered via videotape, the congregational leaders in most small congregations still choose one of the first two of these three options.

Greater Expectations

Perhaps the number-one reason to use the cell phone as a symbol of a new era can be expressed in generational terms. The generations of Americans born after 1960 bring greater expectations to the producers of goods and services than did their parents and grandparents. One consequence is when those higher expectations are met, the next generation projects even greater expectations of the church. One common consequence is the congregation that could compete effectively with other churches in the community for new members back in 1985 no longer is competitive. The average attendance at the weekend worship of God increased by one or two percent annually from 1970 through 1985. For the past decade or two that indicator has been dropping by an average of one or two or three percent year after year.

Each new generation of cell phones has sparked a demand for more and better services. The category has to be expanded and redefined. Another example of that trend has been the public high school. A third can be seen in the design of a "good" single family home, and a fourth is the store selling groceries.

What do people expect to do when they go to church? A few decades ago, as was pointed out earlier, that question could be answered in a couple of paragraphs. The answer in thousands of larger Protestant congregations today often covers pages. That long list may include preparing for a trip as a short-term volunteer missionary to a sister church on another continent; purchasing a book; serving as a member of the team leading worship at one of the five different worship experiences every weekend; helping to staff a Sunday school class for developmentally disabled adults; dropping off a son or daughter at an all-day early childhood development center; learning English as a second language; playing volleyball in the gym in January; parking the car in the church parking lot and taking a shuttle bus to the commuter train; asking the parish nurse to check your blood pressure; participating in a recovery group with those who have experienced the death of a loved one; treating a friend to a cup of coffee in the church's coffee shop; enrolling your first grader in the Christian day school; serving on that team of volunteers committed to building a new worshiping community at this congregation's fourth site located eight miles to the north; sharing in a class of newlyweds on how to build a happy and enduring marriage; fulfilling a court-ordered mandate for forty hours of community service by helping to landscape the grounds; helping to operate the system for videotaping the worship service and editing it to be telecast on the local community access TV channel; receiving competent assistance in preparing your federal income tax returns; participating in a 75–90 minute weekly peer-driven learning experience designed to help couples share their deepest faith questions with one another; attending a class offered by a theological seminary that uses that church as one of its extension centers; playing on one of the six teams in the soccer league administered by that congregation for older children; participating in a mutual support group for recently divorced parents; spending three afternoons every week in activities designed to improve a person's social skills for children who are homeschooled every morning; volunteering two hours a week to help supervise the operation of the skateboard park located on the church property; repairing donated motor vehicles that will be given to single parent mothers who cannot afford to purchase a car; and volunteering to help in sheltering the homeless in the church's fellowship hall one night every week.

Twenty years ago many American adults expressed their identity by their ancestry, where they went on vacation, how they dressed, their level of educational attainment, their hairstyling, or their car or the church or club or civic organization to which they belonged. Today a person's identity often is expressed by the ring tone of their cell phone. Ten years ago parents worried about their teenager who was out driving the family car. Today the cell phone can at least tell them where that family vehicle is and where it is headed. Fifteen years ago the high school student's last chance to check in with a close friend was thirty-five minutes ago in the corridor while changing classrooms. Today's students no longer feel so isolated. If the school does not prohibit cell phones, that instrument makes it possible to exchange messages three or four times every hour. Back in the 1980s a tiny proportion of teenagers had their own landline telephone in their bedroom with their own telephone number. Today cell phones are designed for five- and six-year-olds, but four-year-olds often are placing calls on their siblings' cell phones. Most of these children's great-grandparents, and many of their grandparents, accepted the fact that a home telephone was a luxury they could not afford.

Perhaps the number-one reason for including a chapter on cell phones in this book is discussed in the last chapter. Who has been busy inventing the next phase of the American culture? One answer is the terrorists who have been permeating the American culture with the threat of future terrorist attacks. A relatively tiny number of adults, most of them born after 1950, have motivated the American government to allocate hundreds of billions of dollars to financing a response to this threat.

The combination of the small and relatively inexpensive personal computer, the cell phone, the iPod, and related new "toys" has revolutionized both person-to-person and person-to-institution relationships. Time, physical place, and distance no longer are as restrictive as they were a dozen years ago. The shopper can withdraw cash from a bank account at any time of the day or night without going to the bank or standing in line to talk to a teller. The gambler home alone can play poker at midnight. The half-century from 1960 to 2010 has brought the shift of a large share of retail trade from Main Street to the mall to the big boxes to the cell phone. The investor can buy or sell stocks while sitting in the park and not have to talk with any person. The viewer can watch a television program or a newscast at a time convenient to the viewer. The small congregation in Wyoming averaging two dozen at worship can be inspired and challenged every Sunday morning by the message being delivered via videotape or DVD by one of the top one percent of the preachers in that denomination. The university professor announces, via e-mail to the students, "Wednesday's lecture will be available at eight o'clock Tuesday morning ready to be downloaded into your iPod. We'll discuss it during class time on Wednesday morning." Distance learning has enabled second career adults to earn a degree from an accredited seminary without ever setting foot on the campus of that school. Instead of traveling to the retail store that sold that unwanted Christmas present to your friend, the gift can be swapped or sold via the Web. The couple traveling on Sunday morning to visit a new grandchild can listen to their pastor's sermon, which was downloaded into their iPod while they were packing for that trip. Ten years after the first public worship service, that new mission now averages 12,000 at worship in twenty-eight weekend worship experiences at ten different locations in three states. The founding pastor delivers the message live at two of those twenty-eight services and by DVD at the other twenty-six. Most of those 12,000 worshipers first "checked out" this congregation by visiting it on the Web, by watching a televised service, or by downloading a service into their iPod.

The cell phone is one component of a technological revolution that has given consumers of services, information, entertainment, and goods the power to decide what they want and when they want to receive it. The wireless connection of a growing variety of electronic devices—with the personal computer, the cell phone, and the credit card at the hub of that constellation—gradually had been creating a seamless stream of data, photographs, words, music, and other messages that flow from one machine to another machine. Much of the control that was exercised by the producers of services, information, entertainment, and goods, as recently as the 1980s and 1990s, has been shifted to the consumer. As recently as 2001 newspapers, radio, and television provided journalists with an audience. The emergence of the blogosphere has enabled the bloggers, who once were consumers of the news, to become producers of their version of contemporary reality. Consumers now can be producers. This is one facet of that larger trend called consumerism. In the institutional expression of the Christian faith in America, this trend often is described as "disengagement." Those in the top-down command and control ecclesiastical systems often refer to it as "congregationalism." On the religious landscape it often is manifested in the competition for future constituents between denominational strategies for planting new missions and the new congregation launched by a handful of entrepreneurial individuals who exploit the new technology in designing what quickly becomes a new nondenominational or independent megachurch.

Another expression of an affirmation of the impact of this new technology is the Protestant congregation organized in 1921 that added a second Sunday morning worship service in 1953 and a Saturday evening service, designed primarily for those who have to work or be out of town on Sunday, in 1979. By 1993 those three weekend worship services averaged a combined attendance of 675. The senior pastor retired in 1998. The thirty-two-year-old successor arrived a year later. Five years later the worship schedule included two concurrent services at 9:00 a.m. on Sunday morning followed by two concurrent services at 10:30 a.m., a 5:30 p.m. service followed by a meal followed by a 7:00 p.m. service owned and operated by teenagers and two adults plus a 10:00 a.m. Wednesday morning combination worship service–Bible study largely attended by mature adults living alone, and a 7:00 p.m. Thursday worship service designed primarily for those who will leave town about 5:00 p.m. on Friday. The combined attendance averaged slightly over 1,500 in 2005. The same message was delivered by the same messenger, either in person or by DVD at the Thursday evening service and the first five Sunday services.

A second reason for including this chapter in this book is the cell phone may be the most highly visible symbol in contemporary America of how change creates new choices that increase competition that generates more changes that enhance greater competition that produces additional choices that accelerate the pace of change. The cell phone also illustrates how younger people often adapt to change faster and more easily than do many mature adults. As Robert J. Samuelson has reminded us, the late Ogden Nash may have had the cell phone in mind when he concluded, "Progress might have been all right once, but it's gone on too long."

CHAPTER FOUR

What Are the Consequences of Competition?

For better or for worse, competition in America today is more widespread and more intense than at any time during the past hundred years. That generalization applies to the competition for the best talent every fall among the free agents in major league baseball. It applies to the competition for passengers among the commercial airlines, for customers by retailers, for admission into the top twenty colleges and universities, and to the competition among the manufacturers of new motor vehicles. The competition for the charitable dollar is more sophisticated than ever before. The competition for election to the office of President of the United States in 2004 was a more costly venture than in any previous election. The competition for people's discretionary time among television stations, tourist attractions, newspaper and magazine publishers, professional sports teams, motion picture theaters, state and county fairs, radio stations, service clubs, lodges, and religious congregations is greater than ever before. The competition among tribes of Native Americans to secure a license to operate a casino is an issue no one anticipated back in 1960.

Readers will disagree whether this new era of greater competition began in the 1950s or 1960s or 1970s, but by 1980 policy-makers all across America were beginning to reflect on the impact and consequences of a higher level of competition. From the perspective of the middle of the first decade of the twenty-first century, it may be useful to review several of the more common responses among both profit-driven and non-profit institutions to the impact of competition. Many of the lessons learned in both the profit-driven sector of the economy and by secular nonprofit institutions are relevant to both congregational and denominational leaders as they design ministry plans for the early decades of the twenty-first century.

The Bar Has Been Raised!

Perhaps the most significant impact was discussed in the first chapter. The bar that separates the winners from the losers has been raised. One consequence is a lower tolerance of mediocrity. Another is an increase in the attractiveness of the organizations that are perceived to be winners. A third is a demand for a higher level of customer service. A fourth is many institutions and organizations have to be larger to be able to mobilize the resources required to be competitive.

A fifth is a widening of the gap between the good and the great.

That famous six-word sentence coined by Jim Collins describes how the bar has been raised. "Good is the enemy of great."[1] A shrinking proportion of what often are described as "good churches" are able to compete effectively for the allegiance of younger generations of churchgoers. When policy-makers compromise and agree that "good" outcomes are acceptable, they are lowering the bar. That leads to the road to mediocrity rather than to becoming competitive.

They're Bigger!

For an institution to be able to mobilize the resources to be competitive in today's marketplace, it often has to be far larger than was the pattern a few decades ago. One example is the supermarket designed to sell groceries. A second is the public high school.[2] A third is the motion picture theater. A fourth is the four-year liberal arts college. A fifth is the successor to the "five and dime" variety store of 1955, called the discount store. A sixth is the large medical clinic serving people at several locations has replaced most of the physicians in solo practice.

A seventh is that the average Protestant congregation is more than twice the size it was a hundred years ago. The Census of Religious Bodies of 1906 reported 20.3 million Protestant communicants and members in 194,497 congregations. That produced a (mean) average of 104 members per congregation. Most of these 20.3 million Protestant church members, out of a population of 85 million in 1906, were located outside the very large cities with 300,000 or more residents. By contrast, 57.5 percent of the Jewish members were in those very large central cities as were 28 percent of the Roman Catholics, 25 percent of the Episcopalians, 19.5 percent of the Unitarians, and 34 percent of the Eastern Orthodox.

At the other end of that spectrum 88.6 percent of the Disciples of Christ were members of congregations meeting in places with a population under 25,000 as were 88.5 percent of the Friends, 98 percent of the Mennonites, 86 percent of all Methodists, 87 percent of the Latter-day Saints, 88 percent of all Baptists, 75 percent of all Lutherans, but only 72.5 percent of all Presbyterians, and only 69 percent of all Congregationalists.

The (mean) average membership of the 12,703 Lutheran parishes in the two dozen Lutheran denominations in 1906 was 167 compared to a mean average of 89 for the 64,701 congregations affiliated with one of the fifteen Methodist denominations or 103 for the 54,880 congregations scattered among the sixteen Baptist traditions. The more urbanized Congregational Church reported 700,481 members in 5,713 congregations or a (mean) average of 123 members per congregation. The dozen Presbyterian denominations reported 15,506 congregations with a (mean) average of 118 communicants per church.

At the end of the twentieth century the (mean) average baptized membership of the Evangelical Lutheran Church in America was 475 and 343 for the confirmed membership. For the Presbyterian Church (U.S.A.) the comparable averages were 311 and 226. For the Episcopal Church those two averages were 312 and 246. For The United Methodist Church the (mean) average membership was 235 and 233 members for the United Church of Christ. The African Methodist Episcopal Church reported an average of 403 confirmed members per congregation in 2000.

A Greater Demand for High Quality

An earlier reflection on how the bar has been raised was published in 1982. Thomas J. Peters and Robert H. Waterman Jr. became famous with their book, *In Search of Excellence*.[3]

One way to prevail in a highly competitive context is to raise the quality of the goods and services offered people. That competition over quality in turn has created a consumer-driven demand for even higher quality. That cycle can be seen in motor vehicles, motels, hospital care, the residential halls for undergraduates in colleges and universities, electrical appliances, restaurants, single family homes, hotels, television sets, clothing, public schools, and public highways.

That demand for higher quality, especially from among Americans born after 1960, is reflected in one component of the answer to a frequently asked question. What are the common characteristics of most of the megachurches in contemporary American Protestantism? Six of the most common characteristics are (1) a passion for perfection and quality, (2) a belief system that is proclaimed with clarity and certainty and an absence of ambiguity, (3) relevant messages that address the concerns people bring to church, (4) a surplus of conveniently located and safe offstreet parking, (5) challenging believers to become fully devoted disciples of Jesus Christ, and (6) attractive and challenging opportunities, especially for adult males, to be engaged in doing ministry.

New Players Join the Game

One of the guiding generalizations in the field of planned change is that frequently it is easier to create the new than it is to change the old. Sam Walton began his career as a retailer in 1945 when he purchased a Ben Franklin store in Newport, Arkansas. After five years he and Mrs. Walton decided the most promising way to implement his plans for a new approach to retail trade would be to relocate to a smaller community with an underserved population and little competition where he could create the new. In 1950 he purchased a store in Bentonville, Arkansas. There he began to model a new approach to retail trade. His business model called for making profits from a small markup on a large volume rather than the traditional model of a larger markup on smaller volumes. By 1952 he was beginning to purchase goods directly from the manufacturer, rather than from a wholesaler or via a franchise. That enabled him to expand his business model of small markups in large volumes. The next revision of the business model called for introducing what at the time was a radical change called self-service. Instead of paying sales clerks to wait on customers, the purchasers picked their merchandise and took it to the cashier. (This innovation really traces its creation back to Clarence Saunders in 1916 for his chain of grocery stores.)

The next step was to gradually sever his relationship with the Ben Franklin chain. That relationship peaked in 1968 when Walton owned sixteen Ben Franklin franchises, but in six years dropped to two. He opened his first Wal-Mart discount store in Rogers, Arkansas, in 1962. The business model for that first Wal-Mart store was condensed to four words, "We Sell for Less."[4]

A common parallel in contemporary American Protestantism is the pastor who is invited to come and revitalize what some have diagnosed as a dying church. After a few years of increasing frustration created by resistance to efforts to revitalize a change-resistant institution, that minister resigns. The next challenge for that minister is to plant a new mission. That seventeen-page chronicle of sacred local traditions is replaced by a blank sheet of paper. The crowd of 358 adults at that first public worship service includes no one who can recall "how we've always gathered to worship God in this room at this time of day."

A variation on this model parallels Sam Walton's goal of avoiding the limitations of the franchise relationship. This design calls for a team of three to seven entrepreneurial adults, one of whom may have been ordained years earlier as part of a denominational affiliation, to venture forth and launch a new worshiping community. Instead of the initiative coming from a denominational agency, these are completely locally owned and operated. One expression is the storefront church in the inner city. A second is the house church, many of which are now found in upper-middle-class white suburban communities.

The highly visible third expression of Sam Walton's business model is the team that goes into an underserved community where there is a low level of competition among the churches to serve that growing population and create the new. Walton decided that low price is what consumers are seeking. These new independent or nondenominational megachurches usually base their appeal on nurturing the personal faith journey of adults and teenagers on a self-identified spiritual pilgrimage. Instead of depending on the name of the franchise to attract customers, Sam Walton decided to do retail trade differently than the franchises were doing it. These new and rapidly growing nondenominational megachurches often proclaim, "We do church differently."

Change generates competition and that expands the range of choices available to people. That cycle is the theme of this book. That cycle may begin with any one of those C-words—change, choices, or competition. That cycle is illustrated by the new players in that game called American Protestantism.

One example came following World War II. Several patient but persistent leaders in the Evangelical and Reformed Church, which was the creation in 1934 of the merger of two religious traditions each with a German heritage, and the Congregational Christian Churches, a product of the 1931 union of two American religious traditions, concluded the time had arrived to merge and create a new church. This was viewed by many as a radical change. That proposal generated competition for the loyalty of congregations.

The net result was by the end of 1957 these changes and choices, plus the competition for the allegiance of congregations, had produced three new players for the denominational landscape in American Protestantism. The first was the creation of the Conservative Congregational Christian Conference in 1948. That was followed by the organization of the National Association of Congregational Christian Churches in 1955 and the United Church of Christ in 1957. One plus one equaled three.

The proposed reunion of the northern Presbyterians and the southern Presbyterians was discussed for decades and finally became a reality in 1983. That new denomination is the product of at least ten mergers. When the door was opened to grant congregations choices, one outcome was the organization of the Presbyterian Church in America in 1974 and the Evangelical Presbyterian Church in 1981.

A series of mergers from 1960 through 1987 brought what had been nine Lutheran denominations together to form the new Evangelical Lutheran Church in America. That radical change also granted congregations the right of withdrawal to form new denominations, associations, and movements. That continues to be a work in progress, and it probably will be 2012 or later before a useful count can be made of the new players created by that merger of 1987. Likewise it probably will be 2017 or later before a useful count can be made of the new players on the denominational scene that will be created by the internal competition for congregational loyalty within the Episcopal Church USA or The United Methodist Church. The safe assumption, however, is competition will create the choices required to continue adding new denominations and associations of congregations to American Protestantism.

As new competitors enter the game (that game may be the delivery of health care services, the sale of groceries, early childhood development programs for three-year-olds, commercial air travel, graduate educational opportunities, the production of motor vehicles, a place that provides assisted living accommodations for the fifty-three-year-old widowed parent, the sale of books, or the transformation of self-identified Christian believers into fully devoted disciples of Jesus Christ), many adults find it easy to walk away from the old to help pioneer the new.

One consequence of competition is the arrival of new players. A second is the new players often raise the bar for future players. A third consequence is competition makes it easier for players to switch teams. A fourth consequence may be new sources of conflict. The arrival of ethnic minorities into professional baseball, professional football, and professional basketball illustrates all four of these statements. The arrival of a growing number of very large nondenominational congregations also illustrates all four statements.

Specialists Replace the Generalists

One of the most radical and rapid changes in the United States occurred during the middle third of the twentieth century. The number of one-teacher public elementary schools plunged from 190,655 in 1920 to 149,282 in 1940 to 20,213 in 1960 to 4,146 in 1968. (In 1968 Nebraska led the nation with 1,033 or one-fourth of the total while South Dakota reported 895, Minnesota was third with 499, and Montana was fourth with 298.) In recent years the total number of public elementary schools, grade K up through grade 6 or 7 or 8, has hovered around 62,000 with 3.4 percent reporting an enrollment under 200, 61 percent reported an enrollment between 200 and 699 while 35.5 percent reported an enrollment of 700 or more in 2001. Elementary schools, like farms, teenagers, grocery stores, motor vehicles, and churches are larger than they were back in the 1930s.

One basic generalization is the larger the institution, the greater the proportion of paid staff who are specialists. The teacher in the one-room school of 1936 was a generalist. The music teacher in 2006 is a specialist.

A second generalization is the role of the specialist usually requires more years of formal education than is required for the generalist. That introduces a third generalization. The total compensation for the specialist usually is larger than that received by the generalist. The teacher in 1930 with several years of experience teaching in a one-room country school usually had a high school diploma and perhaps one year of training at the county normal school. That teacher received a cash salary of $500 to $700 for the school year. Fringe benefits such as pension or Social Security or health insurance were not part of the compensation in 1930. After allowing for inflation, that was the equivalent of $7,000 to $9,800 in 2006. That compared to approximately the $46,000 median cash salary for the classroom teacher with seven years of experience in 2006. Specialists cost more than generalists!

The themes of those three paragraphs could be replicated if the focus is shifted to professionals in the practice of nursing or law enforcement or financial services or professional sports or government or law or engineering or the practice of the parish ministry. To meet the challenge to be competitive requires specialized skills, and that costs money.

Competition Brings Denial

What is the impact of increased competition on the policymakers in the institution providing goods or services to the general public? One of the most common responses is denial. Denial takes many forms.

One consequence is the vast majority of Protestant congregations in American Protestantism are too small to be able to mobilize the resources required to attract and serve significant numbers of adults born after 1960. One-half average fewer than 80 at weekend worship. Fewer than 10 percent average more than 350 at weekend worship, and only one in 200 averages more than 2000. For most of the two out of three averaging 125 or fewer at worship, that means carving out a niche based on "what we excel at doing" or affiliating with a missionary congregation or watching their numbers go down.[5]

Should we carve out a distinctive niche or role that differentiates us from other Christian congregations in this community or should we deny that we are no longer competitive?

Denial takes many forms. Fifty years after it was founded as a new mission back in 1954, the leaders of what has become an aging and numerically shrinking congregation decide the time has come to focus on attracting young families. "That was how this congregation got started," recalls one of the younger members of the Long-Range Planning Committee. "My parents were among the charter members. I was twelve years old when we held our first public worship service. If we did it once, we can do it again!"

"Let's see, if you were twelve years old in 1954, that means you were born in 1942. That probably means most of those charter members were adults born in the 1920s or earlier," cautioned another leader. "I'm not sure the strategy that was used to reach people born in the 1920s will work with people born in the 1970s."

"I don't see why not," challenged that ex-twelve-year-old. "If we did it once, we should be able to do it again. If we don't begin to attract younger generations pretty soon, this congregation will fade away. We have to fill that gap in membership now!"

That brief conversation illustrates three expressions of denial. The first is one size still will fit everyone. The use of a rearview mirror in planning for the future is a common form of denial. A second is generational differences are real! Being reared in an era of scarcity is not the same as being reared in an era of abundance. A third expression of denial is this will work because our institutional survival depends on its working.

A more creative response to denial is to flood the system with a mixture of information and persistence.[6]

Competition Builds New Skills

A central theme of this book can be stated two ways. Competition increases choices. An increase in choices erodes old loyalties. One example is the former rural community that has become a part of exurbia. The increase in population density has attracted new congregations. In 1960 seven of the eight congregations identified themselves as three- or four-generation churches. The constituents included children, their parents, grandparents, and several great grandparents. Forty years later several of the children of 1960 are now among the members of a congregation organized after 1980. The woman reared as a fourth generation member of Hope Church married a third generation member of Faith Church. Rather than his joining her church or the wife switching to the husband's congregation, they decided a better way to create a new marriage was to help pioneer a new congregation.

Competition not only increases choices, it also often adds to that list of choices leaving the old to help create the new. One price tag is the erosion of inherited loyalties. One consequence is each time a person abandons the old to become part of the new that increases that individual's freedom and competence to walk away from the old and join the new. What do these have in common? Visiting a foreign country? Writing a book? Switching employers? Getting a divorce? Moving from one state to another state? Committing murder? Getting high on drugs? Trading motor vehicles? Changing from one religious tradition to another? Walking away from an environment filled with internal conflict? The answer is it is easier the second time.

Faster, Better, Cheaper

Competition creates winners and losers. One response is to create a slogan that can serve as both a public relations resource and also describe a new approach to the production of goods or services.

When a denomination plants a new mission, what will be the financial subsidy? A not uncommon practice has been to promise a substantial financial subsidy for operating expenditures for the first year with two-thirds of that amount for the second year and one-third for the third. Sometimes that new mission becomes fully financially self-supporting long before the end of that third year. A more frequent pattern has been the dissolution of that new congregation before its tenth birthday.

That failure rate has generated the creativity required to produce new designs. One design replaced the old model of sending a solo pastor, with the promise of a long-term financial subsidy, to plant that new mission. This new design calls for sending a team of three to seven people, including two to five part-time volunteers, with a larger up-front financial subsidy. Instead of launching a small fellowship with a couple of dozen families, this design calls for an attendance of at least 350 at that first public worship service. It also calls for that new mission to be completely financially self-supporting for both operational and capital expenditures within six months following that first public worship service.

Another design has been pioneered by several nondenominational megachurches. Instead of sponsoring a new mission by sending an associate minister with an dozen families and the promise of long-term financial support, this model redefines the required resources. What should we "export" to create a new worshiping community? The old model called for exporting money, a minister, and several volunteer families. This new model calls for exporting (1) insights, skills, and concepts in "How to do big church in the twenty-first century," (2) two or three paid staff members who have acquired years of experience in how to do big church in a highly competitive environment, (3) a couple dozen volunteers who also have mastered the concepts of how to do big church in a new century, (4) a big chunk of up-front money and, most important, the goal that drives the entire process, (5) a clear understanding that within six months this will be a self-governing, self-expressing, self-financing, and self-propagating worshiping community.

An increasingly popular design calls for abandoning that old model organized around a solo pastor, a potential constituency based on place of residence, and a long-term financial subsidy. This new model calls for that mission-driven single site congregation to become a multisite ministry organized around one message, one identity, one governing board, one ministry staff (that may be designed with one primary messenger or preacher or with a team of three messengers), one budget, one treasury, and an increasing number of weekend worship experiences offered at an increasing number of sites.

All three of these new models illustrate the theme of this book. Competition produces change, and that combination of competition and change expands the number and variety of choices available to people looking for a church home. These three models also illustrate how change and choices raise the level of competition among the churches for future constituents.

The realists will add that one consequence of that increased competition created by change and choices is a new set of winners and a new collection of losers. The economists will explain this book is simply a long essay on the impact of the free market in American religion. Those who have focused on the history of institutions, both profit-driven and nonprofit, in the American culture may object that I have failed to discuss a common alternative created by those three C-words of change, competition, and choices. That alternative is called obsolescence. Fans of space travel will point out I borrowed the subtitle for this section from the National Aeronautics and Space Administration (NASA).[7] They are correct. Back in 1992 Daniel Golden announced that NASA's new goal was to develop a series of spacecraft that would be "faster, better, cheaper." That slogan also has become an important driving force behind ministry planning all across American Protestantism, not simply in new church development.

One operational example of adopting a slogan that combines a response to competition with the central theme of a new ministry plan and also serves as a public relations tool is, "We're here to help you rear your children." Another is, "We do church differently." A third is, "We're here to help you build a healthy, happy, and enduring marriage." A fourth example is, "Our goal is to transform believers into fully devoted disciples of Jesus Christ." A fifth is, "Come join us in changing the world."

The big reservation on this response to competition, as NASA discovered, is that it is easier to create the slogan than it is to fulfill the promise expressed in that slogan. A second reservation is the focal point of that slogan must be customized, not copied.

From Inputs to Outcomes

Those three different models used for creating new worshiping communities introduce one of the most positive consequences of competition. This calls for shifting the focus from input into the system to a greater emphasis on outcomes.

The first of those three models focused on mobilizing inputs into the system. One input was to choose the time and place to plant a new mission. A second may have been to purchase the land for that new mission. A third was selecting the person who would be the mission-developer pastor. A fourth input was the money required to subsidize that effort.

The second model begins with the goal of producing a desirable outcome. That is to create a new self-governing, self-expressing, self-financing, and self-propagating worshiping community as quickly as possible.

This second model also deserves a change in the contents of the reporting system. The old system that focused on launching new churches could emphasize a statement such as this. "Since we adopted our new mission statement ten years ago, we have planted fourteen new missions. Thus far our financial support for these new churches has averaged out to $289,000 annually for the past decade. That also means that over the next decade we will need another $3 million to continue this program."

The new system might report, "Since we adopted our new mission statement ten years ago, we have planted fourteen new missions. Five of the fourteen have achieved that *four-self* goal. The combined average worship attendance of those five was 2,387 this past May. Four of those five are now among the largest 5 percent of the congregations in this judicatory. We expect two others will attain that four-self goal by the end of next year. Four of the fourteen have disbanded. One merged with another congregation of our denomination. The remaining two continue to be subsidized. One of those two should be chartered as an organized church and become financially self-supporting within a year or so. The other one has encountered unanticipated problems, and the future is in question."

That paragraph introduces an extremely valuable tool that is a logical product of placing a greater emphasis on outcomes. This is beginning to have a big impact on denominational agencies as well as congregational life. The common format for this performance audit usually consists of three components.[8] The first states the specific, attainable, and measurable goals in ministry that were adopted earlier for the year just ended. For a congregation these could include the organization of a new adult study group; adding one more worship experience to the weekend schedule; building a continuing relationship with a sister church on another continent; remodeling the fellowship hall; offering two new mutual support groups, one for new mothers and one for recently divorced men; expanding the church-owned parking lot; creating a new ministry with mature adults; and staffing a new ministry with engaged couples on how to create a healthy, happy, and enduring marriage.

The second component of this performance audit focuses on the actual outcomes. What happened? Which goals were attained? Which should be described as "a work in progress"? Which efforts fell short of the goal? Which ones failed?

The third part of the audit usually is the most valuable and the most instructive. This justifies the time and energy required to complete the performance audit. It focuses on two questions. Why? What next? Why did this one meet expectations? Why did the outcomes on that one exceed expectations? Why did each of those two projected outcomes fail to meet expectations? Why were we surprised when the outcomes of those three efforts quickly become success stories, why did they produce desirable, but unanticipated, outcomes?

The other question asks how will what we have learned from this process influence what we will do next? What changes should be made in how we allocate scarce resources (building space, the time of paid staff, the schedule, money, the time and energy of volunteers, et al.) among competing demands. What have we learned that will help improve the policies, goals, and priorities in our ministry plan for the coming year? For the next five years? What are the desirable new outcomes that we can and should include in our planning for the future?

One example of the value of focusing on the desired outcomes and reflecting on the learnings gleaned from that annual audit of performance surfaces when the time comes to seek a successor for the pastor who is about to depart. Rather than look for a successor to fill the vacancy, the emphasis can be on staffing a ministry plan organized around (a) the desired outcomes and (b) the last two or three performance audits. The larger the size of the congregation and/or the greater the competition for future constituents and/or the larger the number of other changes that are anticipated, the more useful it is to focus on desired outcomes from that system rather than concentrate only on new inputs into the system.

Likewise as many denominational agencies are being confronted with a leveling off, rather than a continued annual increase, in their financial resources, one temptation is to focus on increasing dollar receipts. A more productive strategy may combine that annual audit of performance with an effort to agree on the top priorities among the desired outcomes. That introduces another consequence of responding to competition by focusing on inputs rather than outcomes.

The Call to Consolidate

Two of the big retailers in the United States in the 1980s were Sears, Roebuck and Company and Kmart. When Kmart was unable to compete with Wal-Mart and Target, it was forced into bankruptcy. Subsequently the value of the new stock soared as the management sold its best stores and leases. In late 2004 the announcement was made that Kmart and Sears would merge. If you cannot compete, one alternative is to merge.

During the four decades following World War II, that was a response by several smaller Protestant denominations to an increasingly competitive religious marketplace.

The opening of the western frontier after the conclusion of the Revolutionary War created a new era of competition to plant new Protestant congregations. The Methodist circuit rider and the Baptist farmer-preacher represented two of the most aggressive competitors. One of the earliest efforts to reduce competition in American Protestantism came in 1801. The Congregationalists in Connecticut and the Presbyterian General Assembly adopted a plan to cooperate in planting new congregations on the western frontier. "The Plan of Union" attracted the support of other Congregational churches. For more than three decades the Presbyterians and Congregationalists worked in close cooperation in New York, Ohio, Indiana, Illinois, Michigan, and Wisconsin.

One of the unanticipated consequences of this effort to replace interdenominational competition with cooperation was a disproportionately large number of those new congregations chose a Presbyterian affiliation while a relatively small number affiliated with the Congregationalists. That outcome plus the quarrel between the "Old School" and "New School" Presbyterians over control of the denomination resulted in termination of the Plan of Union in 1837.

One of the lessons from that experience is that even though the Presbyterians were clearly the winners in institutional terms, the Old School party saw themselves as the losers in ideological terms. These advocates of orthodoxy concluded that too many of those new Presbyterian congregations were (1) heretical in doctrine, (2) lax in discipline, and (3) not presbyterial in organization. Whether that was the origin of the current rule "Three strikes and you're out!" cannot be verified by this writer. What can be verified from the historical record, however, is that meeting of the Presbyterian General Assembly in 1837 modeled one response to dissenters and heretics. The Old School and the Princeton Seminary group constituted a majority. In addition to terminating the Plan of Union, they expelled four synods, 533 congregations, and approximately 100,000 members. That incident also influenced the outline for this chapter. That explains why this section on cooperation is followed by a section on the competition for control. Both represent responses to competition.

Five decades later a leading urban reformer of that era, Washington Gladden, wrote a series of essays for *The Century Magazine* in 1882–83. He brought an urban perspective, a liberal theological stance, a commitment to efficiency, a passion for ecumenism, and a hostile attitude toward competition to rural America. He and other reformers of that era concluded that rural America was seriously overchurched and underserved. One possible solution would be to encourage small congregations to merge and model their ministry after the large urban congregation. Another was to reduce competition by not planting new missions. A third was to encourage several small churches to come together and form a larger or "cooperative" parish.[9]

In summary, the rational response to competition was for congregations to cooperate in doing ministry. In 1890 several denominations in New England came together to create a comity committee that was designed to minimize competition and encourage cooperation. The rapid growth in the number and variety of "noncooperative" religious bodies and independent congregations since 1960 has undermined the old approaches to comity and cooperation. The most productive, but far more divisive approaches to interchurch cooperation in recent decades have focused on social justice issues such as civil rights, the consumption of alcoholic beverages and tobacco, abortion, war, poverty, human sexuality, the environment, world hunger, ecumenism, children's rights, AIDS, housing the homeless, parental choice in education, law enforcement, terminating the military draft for well-educated young adults, civil liberties, the death penalty, and disaster relief.

Parachurch organizations have been created to fill many of the gaps produced by the decline in interchurch cooperation. In several cases they do compete with interchurch or interdenominational ventures.

The big change, however, has been that the generations who advocated cooperation in the 1880–1960 era have been replaced by younger generations who are more active in the competition for control.

The Competition for Control

Competition produces winners and losers. The winners usually enjoy a supportive constituency who prefer being with a

FROM COOPERATION TO COMPETITION

winner rather than a loser. That usually means a modest level of internal dissent. Most of the constituents, however, tend to be satisfied with the current leadership and with the direction this organization is going. The winners also usually enjoy an increase in both the number of constituents and in the number of discretionary dollars. Happy campers usually are more generous than unhappy campers. Relatively few of the major financial contributors become so discontented they depart.

The losers have problems! One is the demand for resources often exceeds the supply. Another is internal dissent often turns into a struggle over control. This is *not* a new pattern of institutional behavior! It can be seen among the losers all across America: in political parties, in profit-driven corporations, in professional sports, in municipal and state government, and in institutions of higher education. This competition over control also has been one of the longest and most divisive battles in the history of the institutional expression of the Christian faith. One response has been and is majority rule. Another is the persons who have been placed by God in positions of authority should and will decide. The favorite answer for most normal human beings is, "Our side should decide and your side should comply."

During the past four or five decades this competition for control of voluntary associations and nonprofit corporations has been intensified, thanks to the spread of egalitarianism. This is most highly visible among the generations born after World War II.

In a remarkably provocative book, Robert William Fogel, a self-identified "secular child of the Third Great Awakening," has explained how each of the four great religious revivals in American history have stimulated the demand for a greater degree of egalitarianism among the American people.[10] One expression of egalitarianism in recent decades is described as "participatory democracy."[11] A second, which is most strongly urged among black parents of school age children, but has been a part of the American scene since before the Civil War and is increasing among white, Latino, and Asian-American parents, is for greater control over where their children will go to school.[12] Another is the demand for greater accountability by those in positions of authority for their policies and practices. One recent example of that was the creation of the national Review Board for the Protection of Children and Young People in the Roman Catholic Church in America. This group of a dozen Catholic laypersons was appointed to discover why the system of governance in the Roman Catholic Church in America allowed at least 4,392 clerics to sexually abuse more than 10,000 young people over a half century. Why was this allowed to happen? Why were so few priests held accountable for their misdeeds for so long?[13]

The struggle over control in The United Methodist Church has been described as a conflict between the theological conservatives and the theological progressives.[14] From this observer's perspective biblical interpretation is only one of at least a dozen polarizing issues within that denomination.[15] From an institutional perspective the most divisive is over whether to continue the operational policies, practices, and priorities that have produced a major withdrawal of that denomination from the North and West during the last decades of the twentieth century and early years of the twenty-first century. A close second is an internal division over how to fund the employment and retirement benefits promised the clergy. Others will argue the divisions over biblical interpretation, providing jobs for adults, pelvic issues, and the allocation of scarce financial resources are providing the most fuel to feed the fires of competition for control.

By 2005 it appeared The United Methodist Church was ready to turn the pages of history back to 1844 when the 180 delegates to the General Conference met in New York and adopted a Plan of Separation. In 1845 at a special meeting of delegates from the southern conferences they voted by an overwhelming majority to separate. The General Conference of the Methodist Episcopal Church, however, repudiated the Plan of Separation in 1848.

Unfortunately, none of the nine who helped to prepare that Plan of Separation in 1844 are still alive to help design one for the General Conference of 2008.

From this observer's perspective (full disclosure requires a confession that I was not a delegate to that 1844 General Conference), it appears The United Methodist Church currently is confronted with four options.

1. Adopt and implement a Plan of Separation that would offer at least three or four alternatives for each congregation.

2. Continue the withdrawal of this denomination from the religious scene in America.

3. Declare a four-year moratorium on intradenominational quarreling and the competition for control. Order each annual conference to design, adopt, and begin to implement a strategy for fulfilling the underfunded promises to the clergy for employment and retirement benefits.

4. Declare a four-year moratorium on the competition for control and focus on designing, adopting, and implementing a strategy to reverse the withdrawal of that denomination from the 1,500 most populous counties in the United States.

Since most American adults are more comfortable doing what they have had experience in doing, that first option probably would win the most applause but it has too few experienced supporters to be adopted and implemented. The second option of continued withdrawal has the most experienced supporters. If it were combined with the third option for fulfilling underfunded promises to the clergy, that could be a popular compromise. Choosing that combination now also could open the door to designing a Plan of Separation in 2012.

At this point most readers will be asking, "Why devote that much space to the agenda of only one denomination?" The Lutheran, United Church of Christ, and Presbyterian readers may add, "We solved that problem years ago! The egalitarians and the losers in the competition for control have taken their property and withdrawn from our denomination."

Those two comments introduce five reasons for this side trip down the United Methodist road. One is to assure the Episcopalians, "You're not alone. The competition for control is built into the Anglican polity. Remember, it all started with the demand by Henry VIII for control of the church in England."

A second reason is the competition for control can be destructive if the system does not include one or more safety valves. (See chapter 7.) In American political life one safety valve is the third party. In the education of children one safety valve is the private school. Another is homeschooling. The Southern Baptist Convention, the Christian Church (Disciples of Christ), the Evangelical Lutheran Church in America, the United Church of Christ, and most other American Protestant denominations have provided another safety valve. It is called the unilateral right of congregations to withdraw but continue to retain title to their assets. The underfunded promises to the clergy in The United Methodist Church have eliminated that safety valve.

A third reason for chasing that United Methodist rabbit is it illustrates the power of the combination of (a) the potential destructive impact of the competition for control, (b) the continued growth of egalitarianism, (c) the impact of an increasingly consumer-driven secular culture in America, (d) the preference of many adults born after 1960 to help pioneer the new rather than to join and perpetuate the old, (e) the struggle for control which is more likely to be divisive in the institution with a shrinking number of constituents than in the organization with an increasing number of constituents, and (f) the nearly four centuries of an American tradition that suggests it often is easier to walk away from the old and make a new start in a new place rather than stay and attempt to reform the old. That six-part sentence also helps to explain that remarkable increase since 1970 in the number of nondenominational megachurches.

Fourth, this side trip may help to explain why the half-century era of denominational mergers of 1939 to 1987 may be replaced by several decades of schisms in the 1973–2025 era. King Henry VIII has turned out to be only one person in a long procession of Christians who have yielded to the temptation to compete in that struggle for control, and that parade continues to attract new followers.

Finally, after watching this game over control being played on a dozen Christian playing fields in America over the past several decades, it may be useful to compare attendance patterns. The games in which the competition is over control of the denominational system tend to attract a relatively large number of clergy, but tiny numbers of laypersons. The stadiums in which these games are played tend to attract a growing number of players, cheerleaders, coaches, managers, and journalists interested in this sport, but very few fans in the stands. Most of these spectators were born before 1960, and there is a notable absence of teenagers.

The younger generations of American churchgoers, both Protestant and those reared in the Roman Catholic Church, can be found in large numbers in stadiums where different games are being played. One game is called "the search for meaning in life." Another focuses on nurturing the spiritual hunger of self-identified Christian believers on a religious quest.[16] In another group of very large parks the crowds consist largely of people who come because this game is not a spectator sport. It is organized around the transformation of believers into fully devoted followers of Jesus Christ and is designed to attract participants, not spectators. A substantial number of those in attendance were born after 1960, and a remarkably large number were born after 1985. It also is relevant to note that a fair number of younger people go to different games in two or three different stadiums every week, but few go simply to watch the game over control. As pointed out earlier, it attracts players and coaches, but not spectators.

The central theme of this book is competition creates change, change generates conflict, conflict brings new choices, and that cycle generates new competition. That introduces another subsection.

One Consequence of Choosing Up Sides

The history of Christianity in the Western world is filled with accounts of the competition in choosing up sides. One goal is to enlist the most influential players for "our side." Another purpose is the competition helps to distinguish "us" from "them." One way to determine the winner of this competition is to count to see who has the most adherents. The critics of this game explain it is a predictable consequence of original sin.

The history of this competition also illustrates the power of an ancient organizing principle. What is the most effective way to transform a heterogeneous collection of individuals into a closely knit and unified group? For thousands of years the most widely used strategy has been to identify a common enemy and rally the people together to defeat that enemy. The long list of examples includes the devil, Jews, lodges, gambling, war, liberalism, "The Religious Right," slavery, hunger, poverty, the Roman Catholic Church, fundamentalism, heretics, an educated clergy, a false interpretation of Scripture, poverty, denominations, inefficiency, an absence of accountability, tobacco, motor vehicles, clergy-owned housing, alcoholic beverages, the death penalty, the episcopal system of church government, pew rent, and Calvinism. One long chapter in that history is titled "Pelvic Issues" and describes how Christians have decided to choose up sides over such concerns as circumcision, married clergy, artificial birth control, homosexuality, pedophilia, divorce, remarriage after divorce, the ordination of women, dress codes for women, and the authority to spend the money women raise for missions.

The reason for introducing this subject as a consequence of competition is both simple and exceptionally relevant for American Christianity in the twenty-first century. Choosing up sides can be a prelude to a harmless game of volleyball. It also is an easy way to identify an enemy. When that enemy is an external force, institution, idea, pattern of behavior, movement, individual trend, or custom, this can be a useful tactic in reinforcing the cohesion of "our constituency."

When that process of choosing up sides is used to identify an internal enemy, however, that often produces divisive conflict. One current example of that is for more than fifteen years the Roman Catholic Church in America avoided choosing up sides over how to respond to the issue of pedophilia. When that became a public debate in 2001 and 2002, one predictable consequence was the departure of huge numbers of "cradle Catholics." In the nineteenth century when Baptists, Methodists, and Presbyterians decided to choose up sides over slavery, schism was the natural consequence. Choosing up sides over doctrine or the interpretation of Scripture has produced hundreds of schisms.

Currently at least a half dozen of the larger Protestant denominations in America have decided to choose up sides over the same general question. On one side are those who have decided "to go along with and support what headquarters decides." On the other side are those who are opposed to what "headquarters" decides. Some will describe this as the natural consequence of the democratization of American Christianity. Others will add that the process has been accelerated by the growth of egalitarianism. At least a few will diagnose it as the subversion of purpose. As long as evangelism and missions dominate the denominational agenda, the enemy usually will be identified in external terms. When the competition for control moves to the top of the denominational agenda, the natural next step is to identify all internal competitors as "enemies." A common consequence of this battle over control is schism.

Who Will Be the First?

A less threatening consequence of competition has been and is over the adoption of technological advances. Which congregation in this community will be the first to utilize electric lighting? Which pastor will be the first to own an automobile? Which minister will be the first to drive his car on the Sabbath? Which pastor will be the first to proclaim the gospel of Jesus Christ via a local radio station? Which will be the first to install a telephone in the church? What will happen if it rings during worship? Which congregation will be the first to air-condition its meeting place? Which church will be the first to have a paved parking lot? Which preacher will be the first to use projected visual imagery in delivering the sermon? Which church will be the first to own and operate a bus to pick up people and bring them to church? Which will be the first to have the deceased deliver part of the message at the funeral service via videotape? Which will be the first to replace the sermon delivered in person by a live preacher with a videotape of a message prepared earlier and delivered by a person who has never entered that building and make that a standard practice week after week? Which will be the first to have a combination coffee and sandwich shop in the church that will be open to customers at least eighty hours a week?

How have the Protestant churches in America responded to this expression of competition? First, the safe response has been not to be the first, but certainly not the last!

Second, on repeated occasions the impact of technology has brought a change that increased the range of choices available to people. A persuasive argument could be made that the two technological changes that had the greatest impact on American Protestantism during the twentieth century were symbolized by two men. The first was Henry Ford. He began the process that transformed his dream of producing automobiles at such a low cost they would become available to the typical workingman. (Eventually the electric starter made them available to an increasing number of women.)

The second was President Dwight D. Eisenhower who led the effort to construct a national defense highway system that would facilitate the movement of troops and equipment in war time. This evolved into what today is referred to as the Interstate Highway System.

One consequence was the construction of a national network of excellent highways. A second has been a sharp reduction in the number of highway deaths per million vehicle miles driven. Back in 1926 the United States reported 118 traffic deaths for every 100 million vehicle miles traveled that year. The combination of safer vehicles, better roads, and improved law enforcement lowered that rate to 4.9 deaths per 100 million vehicle miles in 1970. By 2005 that death rate had been reduced to slightly less than 1.5 per 100 million vehicle miles.

A third consequence was serious competition for the privately owned railroads for both passenger and freight traffic. A fourth was higher quality raised the bar as drivers told elected public officials what they expected in the quality and safety of city streets and for county and state highways. A fifth has been the average journey from home to work is much longer today than it was in 1950. A sixth has been the sharp increase in the number of families who own two homes—with the second at the lake or in the mountains or in the Sunbelt or near where they went to college.

The combination of the goals articulated by Ford and Eisenhower produced another consequence. This has been the gradual replacement of the small neighborhood general store, motion picture theater, doctor's office, post office, and church by a much larger regional institution.

An equally persuasive argument could be made by old men who were born and reared on a farm. Technology has transformed American agriculture from a labor intensive occupation into a capital intensive industry. The same trend occurred in mining and forestry. One consequence has been the closing or merger of tens of thousands of small Protestant congregations in rural America since 1900.

Educators may point to the yellow school bus that has transformed public education in America. The bus led to the disappearance of approximately 99.5 percent of the one-teacher public elementary schools that existed in 1920.

While it is still a work in progress, technological changes such as the privately owned motor vehicle, better roads, videotapes, low cost air travel via commercial airlines, low cost video conferences, and the Internet have transformed the process of ministerial placement. The parish pastor who retired in 1985 may have spent his entire ministerial career in one or two states. His thirty-seven-year-old grandson or granddaughter who first served a congregation in Pennsylvania later accepted a call to a congregation in Minnesota and is now deciding whether to accept an invitation to move to Florida or to Arizona. One point of commonality is the name of each state ends with the first letter of the alphabet—and that opens the door to future moves to Alabama, California, the Carolinas, the Dakotas, Alaska, Georgia, Indiana, Nevada, Virginia, Oklahoma, Iowa, West Virginia, Nebraska, Louisiana, Montana, or the District of Columbia.

If we reduce the length of the historical perspective in looking at the impact of technology, two trends stand out. The first, which is the theme of this book, is change enhances competition and competition expands the range of choices. The second is the shift in communication from a heavy reliance on the spoken word and printed word to projected visual imagery has transformed what traditionally was described by the word "preaching." The successor word is "message." That represents a switch from a focus on delivery to content. One expression of that is in the thousands of Protestant congregations the successor to the traditional sermon is described as "teaching," rather than "preaching."

Instead of building the identity of a congregation around the ancestry or skin color of the members or the location of the meeting place or the denominational affiliation or the dominant occupation of the members ("the farming community church") or social class or size, this calls for projecting that congregation's distinctive identity around three declarative sentences. "This is what we believe. This is what we teach. This is our specialty." The teaching expresses those three themes. One congregation focuses on persuading nonbelievers on a self-identified religious search to accept Jesus Christ as their Lord and Savior. Another declares, "We're here to help you rear your children." A third emphasizes the quest for social justice as the central theme. A fourth promises, "We're here to help you build a happy and enduring marriage." A fifth explains, "Our purpose is to transform believers into fully devoted disciples of Jesus Christ." A sixth focuses on, "We're here to equip you to do ministry."

A second expression of that focus on content rather than delivery is the reliance on a combination of the spoken word, drama, music, projected visual imagery, personal testimonies delivered via video clips, and closely related peer-driven Bible study groups for delivering that message.

A third expression of this goes back to the point made earlier. The greater the reliance on technology, the greater the demand for specialists rather than generalists. The old tradition projects the expectation that a seminary degree will prepare a Christian believer to fill several roles—preacher, loving shepherd, teacher, administrator, missionary, evangelist, counselor, personal friend, fund-raiser, transformational leader, sacramentalist, and expert on early childhood development. That is a BIG load to place on either one person or on a theological seminary!

One consequence is the emergence of the role of "teaching pastor" who specializes in the preparing and delivering of messages. The Program Director oversees the total ministry while the Executive Pastor is responsible for operation of the institution, and the Minister of Learning Communities has replaced the Director of Christian Education. The media specialist, a musician, a producer, a director, and a scriptwriter work with that teaching pastor on designing the delivery process for the message.

A fourth expression of the impact of this technology is symbolized by Walter Cronkite, Dan Rather's famous predecessor at CBS. Projected visual imagery in general, and television in particular, is not an effective channel of communication for generating loyalty to institutions or products. Television is an excellent channel for building and reinforcing relationships with individuals, but not with institutions.

This first became apparent in the 1930s when commercial motion pictures were designed around one or two star personalities rather than a story line. Radio had begun to exploit this distinction long before television. Franklin D. Roosevelt was one example of how to build a following for a personality rather than for an institution called a political party. A dozen famous radio preachers of the 1930s, 1940s, and 1950s illustrated the same point on the religious scene.

Television came along and reinforced that trend. What is the crucial variable that persuades viewers to trust the accuracy and priorities of that evening network newscast? The name and reputation of the network? The name and channel number of the local affiliate of that television network? The name and reputation of the producer of that news program? Or the personality and tenure of the anchorperson? "Uncle Walter" Cronkite symbolized one answer to that question! The early years of the twenty-first century found CBS, ABC, and NBC all searching for a trusted successor to the twenty-plus year tenure of their aging anchorperson.

One consequence of this shift from a focus on institutions to a focus on personalities was illustrated by the election of the first Roman Catholic to the office of President of the United States of America in 1960. Republicans as well as Democrats voted for John F. Kennedy. The 1990s brought the emergence of a personality who turned out to be a great campaigner in William Jefferson Clinton. This emerging emphasis on personalities also makes it easier to use nicknames. Journalists did not refer to Herbert Hoover as "Herb" or Franklin Delano Roosevelt as "Frankie," but James Earl Carter campaigned as "Jimmy," and Clinton, of course, was referred to as "Bill."

The presidential elections in the United States in 1996, 2000, and 2004 were first of all contests between two personalities. Second, they were contests between who would be more effective in the use of television and the Internet. Third, they were contests between "conservatives" and "liberals." Fourth, they were contests between the two major political parties.

Several decades ago a breakfast cereal named Wheaties attracted purchasers by printing a photograph of a famous baseball personality on each box. That sold more boxes of cereal than did the name of the corporation. That is only one example of how advertising has exploited the tendency of Americans to place their trust in personalities rather than institutions.

One consequence is the public image of Protestant congregations increasingly is in the name of the long tenured pastor rather than in the denominational affiliation of that congregation. Examples include Norman Vincent Peale, Robert Schuller, Rick Warren, Bill Hybels, Adam Hamilton, and Ted Haggard.

Another consequence of television is a shift in responsibilities. In the 1950s it was still widely assumed that churchgoers came to worship carrying an obligation to listen intently to every word in the sermon. Whether that was a valid assumption can be challenged, but many ministers acted on the conviction it was.

Forty years later television had taught tens of millions of Americans that the valid operational assumption was that the person delivering a message carried 100 percent of the responsibility for grabbing and holding the attention of the viewer and listener.

Public elementary and high schools had acted on the assumption that the normal attention span of a child should be at least ten to twenty minutes and fifty minutes for a teenager. Television acted on the assumption that the normal attention span of an adult American varied greatly—from thirty seconds to perhaps as long as five minutes. Those assumptions contrast greatly with the conviction that the oral message delivered by one person standing in one place for twenty to twenty-five minutes should and will hold the attention of the worshiper born in 1980 or 1990 without interruption.[17]

One response is to denounce the impact of television. A second is to change the seating in the room for worship so five to eight worshipers are seated at each of several dozen tables and every few minutes the preacher pauses and raises a question for those worshipers to reflect on briefly with others at their table. A third is to change the pace with an illustration communicated by music or by a projected visual image on a screen or by a brief skit that illustrates the next point or by a videotaped personal testimony of an individual. A fourth response is to deny the impact of television. A fifth is for the resident pastor to prepare and deliver a sermon in person (such as the annual State of Our Church message or in an anniversary celebration) once a year. On all other weekends the message is delivered via videotape or

DVD by someone who combines exceptionally high quality and relevant content with a very high level of competence in oral-visual communication. A sixth response is to switch careers from generalist to specialist.

While not widely discussed, from a congregational perspective three of the most significant consequences of modern technology are (1) the replacement of the small neighborhood congregation by the large regional church, (2) the replacement of ordained generalists by part-time and full-time lay specialists (the majority of whom are women) on the program staffs of the larger congregations, and (3) the raising of the bar on what is graded as "acceptable quality" in the corporate worship of God—the chasm between good and great is wider and deeper today than ever before.

Those three trends help to explain the decrease in the number of Protestant congregations averaging between 100 and 200 at worship, and the increase in the number averaging over 2,000 in weekend attendance. They also help to explain how competition has produced two other changes. A common pattern in the twentieth century was for thousands of numerically shrinking small congregations to choose between two alternatives. One option was to dissolve. The other was to unite with another small church in the hope that merging one noncompetitive congregation with another noncompetitive congregation would produce a competitive church. The new option is to petition to become the "north campus" or "Washington Avenue campus" or the "Cazenovia campus" of a large multisite missionary church.[18]

Another common pattern in the twentieth century was for a large and numerically growing congregation to respond to the shortage of land by sponsoring or "birthing a daughter church." A not uncommon design called for sending the associate pastor, who was an entrepreneurial personality, plus a few dozen of the younger and most venturesome future-oriented families plus some money out to launch a new mission on a larger site at a more attractive location. The "Mother Church" retained the older, tradition-driven members and continued for a decade or two at the "old location." The pastor who encouraged this venture left and was replaced by a successor who agreed with the long tenured pillars, "The reason this congregation is growing smaller and older is Reverend Hutchinson sent all our best young families out to found what has become our number-one competitor for future members."

The replacement strategy for that congregation with limited physical facilities is to raise the ceiling on its potential growth pattern by becoming a multisite church. Instead of exporting staff, members, and money to plant a new mission, it decides to adopt a new role. "We will become one congregation with one name, one message, one staff, one governing board, one budget, one treasury, and one identity with five or ten or twenty or forty or three hundred weekend worship experiences at two or ten or thirty or two hundred locations. We will do that by exporting how to do relevant and high quality ministries with the generations born after 1960." The highly visible current models for this scenario all across America are currently illustrated by colleges, hospitals, banks, supermarkets, universities, medical clinics, theological schools, the YMCA, health clubs, the Roman Catholic Church in America, The United Methodist Church, and scores of nondenominational independent megachurches.

The multisite option is one response to that competition of limited resources and a free market. At the other end of the ideological spectrum is another response.

The Demand for Regulation

One of the most common responses to competition in the American economy has been expressed in a demand for regulation. Tariffs have been and are used to limit competition from imports. Cotton and tobacco farmers sought regulations limiting production. The commercial airlines prospered under regulation.

Members of the United States House of Representatives have used redistricting as a device to create "safe seats" for incumbents. In recent years incumbents seeking re-election have been successful in approximately 96 percent of the contests for House seats.

The 1970s, especially during the tenure of President James Earl Carter, brought the beginnings of widespread deregulation. The advocates of free markets had to agree to some compromises, but deregulation became the dominant trend.

Earlier in the 1940s and 1950s the emergence of large congregations that were not affiliated with one of the mainline Protestant denominations began to erode support for cooperative agreements that would regulate the number and location of both new missions and the relocation of existing churches. This first became highly visible in northeastern Ohio, in the Twin Cities in Minnesota, and in Southern California as well as all across the South.

A few Protestant denominations continue to maintain a system designed to minimize intradenominational competition among the churches but that is rarely mentioned by new members as a factor in their choice of a church home. When asked, "Why did you decide to choose this congregation?" occasionally someone will explain, "We were members of Thusandso denomination, but we were told they could not get permission to open a church here. Since we preferred a church near our home, we chose this one."

The big failure to regulate competition in contemporary American Protestantism can be seen in that growing number of denominationally affiliated congregations that purchase goods and services from parachurch organizations and other "outside" vendors.

A second pattern can be seen in the proportion of the church members' contributions to charitable causes that do not go through denominational channels.

The Demand for Subsidies

Many of the producers of goods and services that are not protected by regulatory measures often are faced with two alternatives. One is to withdraw from that market if they cannot compete. Back in the 1990s, for example, Toys"R"Us accounted for 20 percent of the toys sold in the United States. By the end of 2004 Wal-Mart had 20 percent of that market followed by Target with 18 percent. One alternative was to sell the toys division and concentrate on selling supplies for babies in its Babies"R"Us stores.

Another alternative for those not able to compete in a free market is to seek financial subsidies. Agriculture and commercial air travel are two current examples.

For many years the Roman Catholic Church in America and The United Methodist Church have used denominational systems to channel dollars from the competitive congregations to those that cannot compete. The demand for millions of dollars to compensate plaintiffs who were victims of pedophilia have limited those subsidies in several Roman Catholic dioceses while many United Methodist conferences are facing a financial squeeze as they attempt to fully fund retirement benefits for the clergy. In both of those religious traditions the demands for financial subsidies exceed the supply of dollars.

Redefining the Mission

Back in the 1990s Japan was clearly number one as the leading shipbuilding nation on this planet. By 2004, however, South Korea exported ships valued at over $15 billion and earned the role as the world's leading shipbuilder. The new player in this international game, however, is China. It expects to be number one by 2015. In 2005 South Korea held 40 percent of the market followed by Japan with 24 percent and China with 14 percent as measured by tonnage.

How will South Korea respond to this new competition? First, by expanding its capability to produce steel. Second, by redefining its role. Instead of attempting to compete with the low wage economy of China in building ore carriers, oil tankers, and other bulk carriers, a new strategy has been adopted. The new role calls for the South Korean shipbuilders to specialize in constructing carriers for liquefied natural gas, supervessels that can accommodate 10,000 steel containers and offshore oil platforms.

To continue as a winner in the face of increased competition often requires redefining the role or mission.

Old First Church Downtown was the largest congregation of its denomination in that city in 1948. Among the many characteristics of the membership, one was unique. First Church was the place where the elite met the movers and shakers in the local economy. Thirty-five years later the movers and shakers were living in the suburbs, and First Church had become the fifth largest of the seven congregations affiliated with that denomination in the city. The new senior minister arrived in 1981 and led the process of redefining their mission. Today First Church is the place where adults and teenagers come from a twelve-mile radius to be challenged and equipped to be engaged in doing ministry in the inner city. One of the rewards is meeting other Christian laypersons who also place a high value on volunteering to do ministry. A by-product of that redefinition of mission is First Church currently is the largest congregation of its denomination in that urban county. Another by-product was a tripling in the number of marriage ceremonies held in that building in 2004 over the number in 1985.

The Jefferson Street Church was founded in 1923 as a neighborhood congregation. The masonry building on that one-acre parcel of land was remodeled in 1955. The congregation peaked in size in 1959. The church-owned parsonage was demolished in 1961 to add 17 offstreet parking spaces. The fifth pastor in the congregation's history arrived in 1968 and by 1972 had persuaded the congregation the privately owned motor car was not a passing fad. It was here to stay. A year later an ad hoc Futures Committee recommended the congregation purchase a twelve-acre parcel of land six miles north, construct one large general purpose building on that site, sell the Jefferson Street property, and redefine its role as a regional church. The name was changed from Jefferson Street Church to Hope Church. When that pastor retired in 2003 at age 68, the average worship attendance was seven times the average for 1968. In 1968 two-thirds of the confirmed members were persons born in 1915 or earlier. In 2003 two-thirds of the confirmed members were persons born in 1958 or later.

The redefinition of role opened the door to be able to compete to reach, attract, serve, assimilate, nurture, disciple, and challenge new generations of people.

One response to competition calls for a redefinition of mission and role. Another response requires less creativity and is less productive.

An Increase in the Number of Failed Systems

Instead of adapting to the cycle represented by those three C-words of change, competition, and choices, a widely followed alternative has been to fail. The cemetery that is the final resting place for failed institutions in America now includes millions of graves of retail stores, family farms, magazines, barber shops, book publishers, breweries, elementary schools, religious congregations, manufacturing companies, banks, book stores, commercial airlines, law firms, newspapers, colleges, hospitals, parachurch organizations, blacksmith shops, lodges, theological seminaries, wholesalers, public high schools, gift shops, motels, nursing homes, and other organizations. Given the choice between making the changes required to adapt to a more competitive world, the less creative or less competent often chose to disappear.

That is only one part of the story. The other part lumps together in one category another group that can be described as "failing institutions." In his reflections on his years as the editor of the *New York Times*, Howell Raines lamented the dullness of the newspaper and the "entrenched mediocrity" among the staff. He concluded that while the *Times* "is the indispensable newsletter of the United States . . . a harsh reality of our era is that if the *Times* ever ceased to exist, it would not be reinvented by any media company now in operation, in this country or in the world."[19]

If your congregation as it exists today suddenly ceased to exist, would someone come along to replace it with an exact replica of the current system? If your denominational system suddenly ceased to exist, would someone come along and replace it with an exact replica of the present system?

The early years of the twenty-first century brought an unprecedented public discussion of failed systems in America. That long list includes the failure of huge profit-driven corporations such as Enron, WorldCom, Arthur Andersen, United Airlines, U.S. Airways, and Kmart as well as dozens of defined benefit pension programs, the Montreal Expos baseball team, at least one-fourth of the nation's public schools, thousands of Protestant congregations, traditional department stores,[20] archdioceses of the Roman Catholic Church in America that have been forced into Chapter 11 bankruptcy,[21] the delay of nine years in Florida following the $20 billion damages caused by Hurricane Andrew in 1992 before a more rigorous statewide building code was adopted, the failure of several nation states such as Liberia, the gradual withdrawal of several mainline Protestant denominations from the American religious scene, and the traditional state fair in the Great Plains.

For those interested in learning from the experiences of others, three sets of lessons are easily available.

The most valuable is *The 9/11 Report* issued by the National Commission on Terrorist Attacks Upon the United States.[22] Three different editions have been published. The first sentence of the third paragraph of chapter 11 is worth far more than its weight in gold. "We believe the 9/11 attacks revealed four kinds of failure: in imagination, policy, capabilities, and management." Those four varieties of failure can provide a useful diagnostic outline for evaluating (a) why the membership of that congregation is growing older in age and fewer in numbers, (b) why that successor to the beloved pastor who retired (or died) after an effective ministry over three decades left with a broken heart two or three years after arriving, (c) why that denomination has been experiencing a loss in the number of members, in average worship attendance, in new members received, and in a loss of visibility and impact in the large central cities since 1960, (d) why the merger of those two small congregations resulted, a decade later, in one congregation approximately the same size as the larger of the two, (e) why the proportion of congregational receipts sent to fund denominational budgets has dropped by one-half or more since 1965, and (f) why a disproportionately large number of Protestant megachurches in America were founded after 1965 and are not affiliated with any of the mainline denominations.

A second model was published in 2004 and reported on the failure of the American intelligence gathering system in Iraq.

Another useful investigative report was issued by the Columbia Accident Investigation Board following the explosion of that space shuttle on February 1, 2003.[23] One of the conclusions was the institutional culture of NASA led to flawed decision making.

How does the culture of your congregation influence the policy-making processes in your congregation? Does the culture declare, "We welcome everyone to come and join us every Sunday morning in the corporate worship of God"? How does that inclusive invitation influence the design of your worship services? Is the sermon designed to persuade nonbelievers and skeptics to accept Jesus Christ as Lord and Savior? Or is it designed to transform believers into disciples? Or is it designed to explain to first-time visitors shopping for a new church home, "This is what we believe. This is what we preach and teach. This is what drives the design of our ministry plan. This is how we determine the allocation of scarce resources. This is what you need to know about us before you can make an informed decision about whether this should be your next church home." Or should that Sunday morning worship experience be designed as a bilingual experience in order to welcome both those who prefer to worship in English and also those who prefer to worship God in Spanish or Korean or Mandarin or German?

Likewise, is the system your denomination uses to fund denominational budgets appropriate for the American religious culture of 1956 or 2006? Is it designed to be competitive in the pursuit of charitable contributions in the twenty-first century? If it is a top down command and control system, will that be effective in reaching and attracting the millions of egalitarians born in America since 1950?

An interesting and provocative reflection on how a failing institution responded to the arrival of a new leader who came as a self-identified "change agent" was written by a former Executive Editor of *The New York Times*.[24]

The BIG recent development is that much of the analysis—and much is seriously uninformed—of failing institutions in America is now circulated by bloggers on the Internet. How are the bloggers on the Internet evaluating your denominational system? What will be their impact in the early years of the twenty-first century?

The response to that question will depend to a substantial degree on (a) what the denominational system relies on as the important criteria in the self-evaluation process and (b) what the bloggers count. That, however, requires an analysis that cannot be undertaken before we have more experience with the impact of the bloggers on Christianity in America.

While this is far from a comprehensive discussion of all of the impact of a culture and economy that is far more competitive than it was in the 1940s and 1950s, it does introduce two concluding observations. The first is a shift from continuity to discontinuity. For centuries Western civilization was marked by long eras of continuity with the past.

One example of that in the history of the United States of America was in responses to changes in the economic cycle. From 1800 through 1945 adjustments in the economy produced one of three outcomes. One was an era marked by inflation. A second was a period of deflation. The third was a period of stability. When 1967 is used as the base year or reference point, the Consumer Price Index stood at 100 compared to 31 in 1800. During the nineteenth century it fluctuated between 55 in 1815 and 25 in 1900. Between 1900 and 1945 it fluctuated between a low of 24 in 1900 and a high of 60 in 1920. In 1917 that indicator stood at 38.4, the highest since the late 1860s. In 1921 it was at 53.6 and a low was reached in 1933 at 38.8, the same level as back in 1827. For 1945 it was back up to 54. A new all-time high of 67 was reached in 1947. Twenty years later in 1967 a new high was reached at 100. The following dozen years brought a doubling to 217 in 1979 and doubled again to 434 in 1993. A reasonable guess is that by 2007 the Consumer Price Index will be at least six times the 1967 level.

That trend symbolizes the discontinuity in most other facets of the American culture since the end of World War II. Other examples include agriculture, manufacturing, the sales of groceries, higher education, the delivery of health care, communications, transportation, entertainment, the role of the mainline Protestant denominations, and the length of the journey from home to work or to church.

One common consequence is when the head honcho (governor, manager, bishop, chief executive officer, president, board chair, mayor, pastor, executive director, coach, or cabinet secretary) departs, that should *not* trigger a search for a successor. Instead the first step is to design a new corporate strategy or to redefine the primary constituency or to agree on a new statement of the mission or to conduct a comprehensive audit of performance or to agree on a new set of desired outcomes. That may be followed by a restructuring of what has become a dysfunctional organizational system. After agreement has been reached on the plan, the search begins for the leader who can lead in the implementation of that plan or strategy.

An alternative is to begin by seeking a leader who will fill the role as an agent of planned change initiated from within an organization. That visionary leader will be expected to lead the process of redefining the role and designing the staff configuration required for fulfilling that new role.

The Call for Visionary Leadership

In summary, one of the most significant consequences of competition frequently is an increase in discontinuity with the past. The midsized or small neighborhood congregation needed a pastor who was an extroverted personality and excelled in the role of the loving shepherd. When the decision was made to relocate the meeting place and become a large regional church, that represented great discontinuity with the past. One common predictable consequence was the loss of

15–30 percent of the members. Another consequence was the need to redefine the role of pastor from congregation-builder to kingdom-builder.

The central distinction is between (a) the people who are searching to fill a vacancy with a leader who will come and recreate 1955 or 1985 and (b) those who have designed a plan to create a new tomorrow and are seeking a leader who can help create the new. The demand for those who can recreate 1955 or 1985 exceeds the supply by perhaps a 5,000 to 1 ratio. While the demand for those who bring the gifts, skills, experience, commitment, and vision required to create a new tomorrow is less than the demand for those who can recreate or perpetuate the past, the demand exceeds the supply by at least a 5 to 1 ratio.

The good news on this subject is in that rapidly growing supply of research on both failures and successes that can be a tremendous resource for those willing and able to help an organization become more competitive tomorrow than it was yesterday. One useful reference that speaks to leaders in non-profit organizations is chapter 11 of *The 9/11 Report* referred to earlier.

An exceptionally relevant essay for denominational executives or for the recently arrived senior minister of the large Protestant congregation was written by Peter Drucker.[25] The second paragraph summarizes the eight practices followed by what Drucker found to be the most effective leaders. Drucker's "bonus" or ninth recommended practice is "Listen first, speak last."

This demand for transformational or visionary or strategic leadership illustrates the central theme of this book. Change creates discontinuity, which raises the level of competition that leads to more choices, and an increase in choices generates greater competition.

How that process will be described and evaluated will depend on what the policy-makers decide to count.

CHAPTER FIVE

What Do You Count?

T his chapter rests largely on five basic assumptions about
life in America in the twenty-first century. First, we count
what we believe is important. The future-oriented three-
year-old with four older siblings counts birthdays. The worried
wife with a husband in intensive care counts the hours he has
been in a coma. Since being diagnosed with glaucoma, I await
the periodic count that tells me the pressure in each eye.

Second, what we count becomes important. The pastor who
requests an usher count of worship attendance every week usually believes a 10 percent increase or decrease over the same
Sunday of that month a year earlier is an important indicator.
The teenager looks to the future when celebrating that sixteenth
birthday while the grandparent looks to the past when celebrating a seventy-sixth birthday. The denominational official who
believes a central responsibility of congregations is to collect and
send dollars to headquarters to fund denominational budgets can
explain why those counts are given high visibility in those
monthly newsletters sent to every pastor. Many retirees want an
accurate count of inflation over the past twelve months because
that will determine the increase in their Social Security check.

The third assumption is there is a vast difference between
placing a high priority on counting inputs into the system and
counting outcomes produced by that system.

A fourth assumption focuses on the process. Does it produce valid and meaningful indicators that accurately describe contemporary reality? For example, what is the divorce rate in the American population? A widely used process comes up with the answer of 50 percent. Each year the National Center for Health Statistics reports the number of marriages and divorces for the previous year. These also are converted into rates per 1,000 population. In recent years there have been approximately 7.5 marriages and 3.8 divorces per 1,000 population. The obvious conclusion is the divorce rate is 50 percent—one divorce for every two marriages.

The fallacy is the people getting married in any one year have nearly a zero overlap with those being divorced in that same year. The reports are measuring two separate population cohorts. Since a disproportionately large number of people being divorced in any one year already have been divorced at least once, that also distorts the divorce rate.

A better approach calls for a more precise wording of the question. What proportion of the American population who have ever married are still in their first marriage? For obvious reasons the rate goes down as the number of years of being married rises, but only to a point. One recent survey revealed that the highest divorce rate in 2001 was 41 percent for men born in the 1942–51 era. Among women born in those years who had ever married, 39 percent had been divorced at least once. Demographers who have studied this subject agree the divorce rate peaked at about 41 percent of all marriages and is declining. One reason is the increase in the proportion of the American population who have graduated from college. Over a lifetime the divorce rate for all college graduates who marry is about one-half the rate for those who did not graduate.[1] An overlapping explanation is the divorce rate is higher among people who marry before their twenty-first birthday than those who marry later.

Is Membership a Useful Indicator?

A widely used approach to evaluating congregations relies on changes in the membership. The typical survey lifts up three common patterns. One is a series of short pastorates of two to seven years is more likely to produce a decrease in membership than is a series of pastorates of fifteen or more years. A second is the longer the congregation has been gathering in the same room to worship God, the more likely that congregation will report a decrease in membership. A third is over a five-year period approximately one-third of congregations report a decrease in membership, one-third to one-half are on a plateau in size, and close to one-third experience an increase in membership.

How useful are those numbers? One reason to challenge the use of membership numbers is the huge variation in the criteria used to define membership. Two congregations affiliated with the same denomination meet in buildings six miles apart. Both were founded before the Civil War. During the past five years one experienced an increase in membership from 1,533 to 1,587, but a decrease in average worship attendance from 491 to 453. The other reported a decrease in membership from 937 to 865, but an increase in average worship attendance from 672 to 845. Which is the larger of these two congregations? Which is increasing in size?

A second reason for skepticism about the relevance of membership data is that a large proportion of Americans born after 1950 who are not joiners. They display a lower level of interest than did their parents and grandparents in joining lodges, political parties, veterans' organizations, religious congregations, and service clubs.

A third reason is that growing number of nondenominational congregations that simply do not have a membership roster or restrict membership to a relatively small number of deeply committed and heavily involved participants. They welcome everyone to "Come worship with us," but have a high threshold into membership and only members are invited to teach or to serve in policy-making positions.

A fourth reason emerged out of that sharp increase in the number of "Cradle Catholics" who now are regular worshipers with a Protestant congregation. Rather than offend their parents by terminating their membership in that Catholic parish, they choose the roles of worshiper and learner, but do not seek to become members. That also eliminates another potential problem in those congregations that affirm believer's baptism and reject the baptism of infants.

A fifth and overlapping assumption that is a part of the foundation for this chapter takes us back to the central theme of this book. What is the worldview that drives the decision as to what should be counted? If the planning process is driven by the assumption there is a shortage of resources in that organization and/or by a focus on producer-designed services, a normal, natural, and predictable approach will be to count inputs into the system. If, however, that planning is driven by a desire to be able to compete effectively with other producers of similar services and/or to expand the customer base, the logical focus will be on measuring outcomes produced by that system.

One widely publicized example of these two approaches came in the commercial airline industry following September 2001. United Airlines and Delta Airlines counted inputs into their systems. Both counted the number of dollars paid each pilot every month. Since a bigger number clearly is a better number than a smaller number, both came out of September 2001 with a salary scale twice that of Southwest Airlines. The discount carriers such as Southwest Airlines and Jet Blue have focused on outcomes produced by their system. Both counted the number of passengers they carried each day. Both concluded a higher number was a better number than a lower number. Both concluded one way to cultivate customer satisfaction is lower fares. A second is direct flights that do not call for changing planes. Both concluded it was better to give higher visibility to an outcome of their system, lower fares and direct flights, than to any input into their system such as the salary scale for pilots. When the time comes to purchase an airline ticket, many Americans will give greater weight to the price tag on that ticket than they give to the salaries paid the pilots.

Six Critical Questions

One divisive issue in designing a self-evaluation process for either denominational systems or for congregations surfaces repeatedly. If both denominations and congregations are affirmed as part of God's creation on this planet, is it appropriate for sinful human beings to attempt to evaluate what is happening in

God's creation? Or is the goal that all outcomes will be evaluated by only one criterion—is that outcome pleasing to God?

One response is to avoid that doctrinal debate and begin with the fact that every week all across America congregations are being evaluated by first-time visitors who come with one question, "Is this the church for me?" Instead of being guided by the denominational affiliation many of those visitors ask, "Will this church feed my spiritual hunger?"

Likewise denominational systems are being evaluated by both outsiders and insiders. Therefore the critical question is *not* whether evaluation should be allowed. The nature of the highly competitive ecclesiastical landscape in America has created a climate for evaluation.

That introduces the second of these six questions. What should be counted? Should the focus be on measuring inputs into the system? Or on measuring outcomes? The producer-driven culture usually measures inputs into the system. The consumer-driven culture measures outcomes. How will that Sunday morning worship be evaluated? Was it well designed? Was it designed as a presentation-type service? Or as a participatory experience? Was it pleasing to God? How many of those present dozed off during the sermon? How many left saying to themselves, "I'm glad I came today! I now have a better and more meaningful understanding of the grace of God." How many left planning to go elsewhere to worship next week?

That raises the third question. What are the criteria or indicators that will be used to evaluate the outcomes? What criteria will be used to measure inputs into the system? Which indicators will be given a high value by the producers?

Which indicators will be given a high value by the consumers?

"We love our pastor! Our pastor is a deeply committed Christian who is always available to people and radiates God's love. I've been a member here for nearly thirty years, and this is the first time we've ever had a pastor who has earned the respect and support of every member."

"In the seven years since our current pastor came, our church attendance has doubled, the median age of our members has dropped substantially, and dozens of lives, including my own, have been transformed by our involvement in outreach ministries."

Which of those two comments is most compatible with the goals of your congregation? What do you count as you evaluate the ministry of your pastor?

A fourth question is who defines these criteria for evaluation? Who decides what to count? One source of intradenominational conflict emerges when denominational officials use a different set of criteria for evaluating the performance of congregations than are used by the local leadership. Likewise a source of intra-congregational conflict that can be highly divisive surfaces when the pastor uses one set of criteria, the volunteer leaders use a different set, and many of the laity rely on a third set. The road to harmony requires we all agree on what we count. Dollar receipts? Worship attendance? Expenditures? Unhappy members? Sunday school attendance? Apathy? The number of youth in worship? The increase or decrease in the size of our mortgage? The proportion of our total financial receipts that are sent to denominational headquarters? The number of baptisms? The number of our people who have spent at least ten days during the past year as short-term volunteers working in ministry with fellow Christians in a sister church on another continent? The increase in the number of church-owned parking spaces? The number of conversions? Easter attendance? The number of new members received last year? Staff turnover? The number of lives that are being transformed through the ministries of this church? The number of people who have switched their allegiance to another church in this community?

This usually is much less of a problem in that megachurch organized back in 1982 where the founding pastor (a) wrote the rule book that includes a high degree of compatibility between purpose and what is to be counted in that annual audit of performance and (b) continues in office as the current senior minister and as the number-one interpreter of that rule book.

A fifth question looks at the world from another perspective. It can be summarized in four words How do we compare? The pediatrician weighs and measures the baby and explains, "Compared to other six-week-old babies, this child is at the 87th percentile in length and the 85th percentile in weight." The father of three children ages 22, 19, and 17 recalls; "I can remember when I was the tallest person in our family. Now I'm the second shortest." The pastor of the congregation averaging 120 at worship explains to the governing board, "Since we're larger than two out of three congregations in American Protestantism, we should be planning and acting like a big church, not a small congregation." A study in 2002 by the National Institute on Alcohol Abuse and Alcoholism reported approximately 1,400 college students, age 18 to 24, die annually as a consequence of alcohol abuse, mostly from traffic accidents, but at least 300 die from drowning or alcohol poisoning. Of the 100 coldest large cities in the United States, Canada, and Russia that also have a population of 100,000 or more, five are located in the United States, ten in Canada, and 85 in Russia. In seven of the ten years between 1991 and 2000 our regional judicatory reported a loss in membership, but in four of the five past years, the combined total average worship attendance increased by at least 2 percent over the previous year. "Back in 1980 when I came as your new pastor, this was the seventh largest, using average worship attendance to measure size, of the twelve Protestant congregations in this town. Thanks to the population growth, there are now nineteen Protestant churches within the city limits. Last year our average worship attendance placed us sixth among those nineteen in size and we ranked fourth among the eleven of the twelve that have survived since 1980." In 2002 the city health officials of New York City estimated 2,500 died of influenza but death certificates for that year listed only two deaths from influenza, up from zero in 2001. For most of the other 2,500, pneumonia or heart disease was listed as the cause of death.

Do we compare ourselves with others? Or do we combine our performance with the past? Or do we combine those two to compare with both our past as well as with others?

Finally, what do you count in the system of accountability that is used in the annual audit of performance? What do you count in defining contemporary reality for your congregation, or denomination, as you design a ministry for the next five to seven years? Does the wording of the questions asked in this self-evaluation process focus on the most relevant measurable outcomes? As you seek to reach agreement on the desired outcomes in that ministry plan, what do you count?

A common pattern in contemporary American Protestantism is for newcomers to become regular participants in the weekly corporate worship of God, but they never ask to become full members. What do you count to measure growth? Membership or worship attendance? Membership or the transformation of lives?

A Denominational Perspective

While the differences in the criteria used to define the term "member" make it of limited value in comparing one congregation with another church, membership can be a useful indicator in those denominational systems that have a long history of using the same categories in collecting data from congregations. The annual increase or decrease in the combined membership of all affiliated congregations usually will rank no higher than thirteenth among the most useful of the self-evaluation questions that include membership as an indicator.

1. Has the median membership of all affiliated congregations been increasing or decreasing? This may be the quickest and simplest way to begin to answer the question, "Is our denomination competitive today in the quest for future constituents?" (A better question substitutes average worship attendance for membership in this question.)

2. What was the combined total number of new members received by affiliated congregations last year?

3. How does that total compare with each of the past dozen years?

4. What was the ratio of average worship attendance to membership for all affiliated congregations last year?

5. How does that ratio compare with the ratio for the past dozen years?
6. What was the combined total number of new members received last year by baptism and/or profession of faith?
7. How does that number compare with each of the past dozen years?
8. How many new members were received by affiliated congregations by intradenominational letters of transfer? (When translated into new members received by intradenominational letters of transfer per 1,000 members, that rate can be a useful indicator of the capability of your denomination to retain the allegiance of members. How does the rate for last year compare with the retention rate for 1955? For 1975? For 1995? For 2005? This yardstick for measuring retention suggests a rate of 25–40 per 1,000 members is above average, a rate of 15–25 is average, and a rate below 15 per 1,000 members raises serious questions about the capability of the congregations in that denominational system to retain the loyalty of the constituents. This indicator is of far less value when used by individual congregations. A rate of 25–40 per 1,000 members may be a product of (a) a focus on ministry with members born before 1940 who tend to display a high level of denominational loyalty and/or (b) the influx of new members from a nearby sister church in the same denomination that is polarized by internal conflict and/or (c) excellent facilities at a superb new location with an abundance of offstreet parking and/or (d) an exceptionally high quality weekday ministry with children.)
9. What was the proportion of affiliated congregations that reported fewer than 100 members last year? How does that proportion compare with previous years? If that percentage has been increasing, what is the explanation? (If that proportion is higher than 30 percent, that should be a source of concern!)

10. What was the proportion of affiliated congregations that reported a membership last year of 500 or more?
11. How does that compare with previous years? In an era in which many institutions in the United States have to be large in order to mobilize the resources required to be competitive that proportion should be (a) increasing every year and (b) above 20 percent.
12. What proportion of all affiliated congregations that have been worshiping at the same address since before 1970 reported an increase in membership? What proportion of all affiliated congregations that have been worshiping at the same address for fewer than twenty years reported an increase in membership? What does a comparison of those two sets of numbers suggest?

Checking Out the Competition

A widely used criterion for evaluating the performance of investor-owned and profit-driven corporations in America is to compare one company with its competitors. This process often uses indicators such as total receipts, profits, employees, and market share.

An increasing number of larger Protestant denominations and congregations are now comparing their annual audit of performance with their competitors. One big source of opposition to this is the plea that Christians should be cooperating in ministry, not competing. One major barrier is the absence of common definitions of categories. It is unrealistic to compare membership statistics, for example, of the congregation that has a low threshold into full membership with the congregation that has a high threshold and requires one year of regular participation in the weekly corporate worship of God before being eligible to apply for admission into a class for prospective future members.

One common approach is to offer this trade. "We are seeking to learn how our congregation ranks in size, using average worship attendance as the yardstick for measuring size. If you will mail us your average worship attendance for your most recent twelve month period on the enclosed postcard, we will send you

FROM COOPERATION TO COMPETITION

the data we collect from all the other Protestant congregations in this community who reply to this request."

The second year of this process usually produces responses closer to 100 percent coverage than does the first year. That simple process enables the leaders to "see how we compare with our competitors."

A more widely used, and a more subjective, process requires each member of the governing board to either (a) worship with two other competitors on a typical Sunday morning every year or (b) spend at least three hours by appointment every year with the pastor and/or program staff members of each of two competitors sharing information and plans on ministry for the future. This is based on the assumption that a sharing of information with the competition can be a productive learning experience.

These two options, of course, are completely irrelevant for those who are convinced Protestant congregations in America should not and do not compete with one another in the quest for future constituents. Those skeptics, however, should not be reading this far in this book!

The Big Divide

Finally, we come to what may be the highest wall of demarcation between two of the parties in this discussion on the criteria for self-evaluation. On one side are those who are convinced (1) Protestants should cooperate, not compete, in ministry, (2) the rich should help the poor, (3) the strong should help the weak, (4) membership trends are the best single indicator of progress or absence of progress, (5) academic credentials are more valuable than ever before, and (6) every congregation should design its own ministry plan as an expression of its autonomy.

On the other side of this line are those who argue there are only four or five really useful criteria in determining which Protestant congregations will be competitive in the quest for future constituents in twenty-first-century America. The first is an expansion of the nineteenth century concept that influenced English, American, and German missionary efforts. The original model called for every congregation to be self-governing, self-financing, and self-propagating. In the twentieth century that three-self principle was expanded to self-governing, self-expressing, self-financing, and self-propagating. From this traveler's perspective that is the best single yardstick for predicting which congregations will be competitive in American Protestantism in 2025 or 2050.

The second most relevant criterion can be summarized in the word "passion." The leaders, both clergy and lay, are driven by a passion to fulfill the Great Commission. A third yardstick is the message, "This is what we believe, this is what we teach, and this is what defines our priorities on what we do and why we do it," articulated with certainty, clarity, and an absence of ambiguity. A fourth criterion is relevance. Like beauty, that is in the eye of the beholder. A fifth useful predictor of what the future will bring is quality. There is an unprecedented demand for quality all across the American landscape today. The rise in the level of competition among the producers of goods and services is one explanation for the increase in that demand.

A sixth criterion is the central theme of this book. Which congregations will be the most effective in reaching, attracting, serving, assimilating, nurturing, discipling, challenging, and equipping for ministry the generations of Americans born after 1960? Those that recognize that (a) change is a requirement for being competitive, (b) conflict is a natural by-product of change, (c) competition stimulates creativity, (d) creativity generates new choices, and (e) increasing the number and variety of choices creates a demand for additional change. The road into the twenty-first century is a path marked by greater competition for the time, loyalty, energy, creativity, money, and participation of younger generations. That is a steep and uphill road, but the other option, the downhill road, terminates at a place called institutional obsolescence.

CHAPTER SIX

What Is a Stability Zone?

A pproximately 30 percent of the 41,000 congregations affiliated with the Southern Baptist Convention were experiencing numerical growth in the 1998–2003 era. Nearly one-fourth were declining, and 46 percent were on a plateau in size. Those numbers were the product of a study conducted by Bill Day at the New Orleans Theological Seminary and completed in late 2004.[1]

When the definition was redefined to identify a "healthy and growing" congregation, the criteria were expanded to four:

1. An increase of at least 10 percent in the total membership over the past five years.
2. At least one baptism in both the first and last of those five years.
3. A membership to baptism ratio no higher than 35 to 1 in the fifth year.
4. Conversions accounted for at least one-fourth of the net membership growth in that fifth year.

Using those criteria, Dr. Day found only 11 percent of all Southern Baptist congregations qualified as "healthy and growing."

One interesting facet of that report is an earlier study by LifeWay Christian Resources reported that for the 1978–83 period: 30 percent of Southern Baptist congregations were experiencing numerical growth, 18 percent were in decline, while 52 percent were on a plateau in size.

Those patterns resemble the trends in at least a dozen of the larger Protestant denominations in America. Depending on the definitions used to define these categories, approximately 15–35 percent of all Protestant congregations are experiencing sustained numerical growth while approximately one-third or more have been on a plateau in size for several years and another third to half are declining in size.

In the search for explanations, one road leads to an examination of correlations. One correlation is with the number of years that congregation has been gathering at the same address to worship God. If that time period exceeds 30 years, that increases the probability the congregation is experiencing numerical decline.

Another correlation that appears repeatedly is size. In a comprehensive study published on May 8, 2001, that covered the 1994–99 period and uses average worship attendance to measure size, Richard P. Deitzler found a consistent pattern. Among the 24,749 United Methodist congregations reporting an average worship attendance under 100 in 1994 a total of 60 percent reported a lower average worship attendance for 1999. At the other end of the size spectrum of the 2,859 United Methodist congregations reporting an average worship attendance of 250 or more in 1994 a total of 68 percent reported an increase for 1999. The typical change was an increase of at least 25 in attendance.

A variety of other studies report a positive correlation on pastoral tenure. A disproportionately large number of the congregations averaging more than 800 at worship have enjoyed the leadership of the same senior minister for at least two decades.

A Denominational Perspective

Why do only a small minority of the small and midsize congregations in American Protestantism that have been meeting at the same address for three decades or longer report they have been enjoying sustained numerical growth? Why do two-thirds or more report they have either been on a plateau in size or experiencing a decrease in their constituency?

Why do the proposed changes required for the congregation on a plateau in size or shrinking in numbers to be able to attract more new constituents frequently generate internal conflict rather than enthusiastic support? What can be done to reduce the probability that a by-product of change will be conflict?

One explanation is the theme of this book. Most congregations have been either unwilling or unable to make the changes required for them to be able to compete for the allegiance of the potential new constituents required to replace those who leave plus the additional newcomers required to produce a pattern of net numerical growth. In simple terms one reason several denominations are experiencing numerical decline is because most of their affiliated congregations are not competitive. Catching up with the competition is more likely to create internal conflict than eager support for change!

That raises a related question. What can a denomination do to increase the proportion of congregations that are able to reach, attract, serve, assimilate, nurture, challenge, and disciple adults who may be searching for a church home? One strategy is to plant new missions designed to attract people who want to pioneer the new. Another is to encourage and resource the emergence of a larger number of large congregations. A third is to encourage longer pastorates. A fourth is to encourage and resource congregations meeting in what has become a functionally obsolete building on an inadequate site at a poor location to relocate to better facilities on a larger site at a more attractive location.[2]

A related explanation is the level of competition has been raised. This is most obvious in those communities that have been experiencing a rapid increase in the number of residents. The resources and leadership that enabled a congregation to compete for future constituents in 1957 is not adequate for today's more competitive religious landscape. One reason is inherited denominational loyalties were a central factor in why people chose a particular congregation in 1957. For most Americans born after 1960 that is now a minor variable.

The Larger Context

For those willing to move from the objective to a more speculative analysis, a useful question is why are so many Protestant congregations unable to make the changes required to be competitive on today's religious scene? A parallel question is why don't horses fly? The obvious answer is horses were designed to walk, not fly. Two-thirds of all Protestant congregations in America average fewer than 125 at worship. Most of these have been in existence since before 1975. Gradually the top six priorities have evolved so today that agenda includes (1) gathering together every week for the corporate worship of God, (2) taking good care of today's members, (3) transmitting the Christian faith to children, (4) maintaining the real estate, (5) collecting and sending money to hire others to do ministry on their behalf, and (6) taking good care of "our Pastor."

Lest this discussion be diverted by those who want to focus on how a congregation can be organized around worship, evangelism, learning, missions, and fellowship, we need to look at three other parts of the larger context.

The first is to recognize that for many adults life today is filled with stress, disappointments, pressures to accommodate to change in the workplace, family problems, the polarization of life over a variety of divisive issues, and unanticipated surprises. Back in 1970 a book by a futurist, Alvin Toffler, was published. The theme was to help people prepare for life in the twenty-first century.

One of the points Toffler makes is to affirm the value of the "personal stability zone."[3] When confronted with the rapid pace of change, many people feel a need for the comfort and stability of "enduring relationships." The baby clings tightly to its mother when confronted by a stranger. That fast-paced family vacation ends with a sigh of relief and the comment, "It's sure good to be home." The coming of Monday morning is less stressful if the workplace resembles a comfortable stability zone.

A brief glimpse into the life of Michael and Karen Lancaster will illustrate a few of the characteristics of a stability zone.

They were married in 1996 and now have two children. Emily is six, and Jacob is three. They gather around the dining room table for a meal a dozen or more times every week. Karen and Michael sit facing one another across the table. Three-year-old Jacob sits in a chair to his mother's right while Emily sits across the table to her father's right. One evening Michael arrives at the table first and sits in the place normally occupied by Jacob. Is this a game? Or is Dad determined to destroy a stability zone?

The following Sunday morning the Lancasters go to church. Three-year-old Jacob looks forward to a stability zone called the nursery. Emily eagerly goes to a stability zone called the first grade Sunday school class. First graders have been meeting in that same room since 1987. The parents go to the same stability zone to be with the same people they have built up enduring personal relationships with since they joined that congregation in late 1999. This class was organized in 1997 and has been meeting in the same room every Sunday morning since 1998. More than one-third of today's members helped organize it back in 1997. It usually takes Michael and Karen seventeen minutes to leave this stability zone, pick up Emily, chat with friends, and move on to their second stability zone called the sanctuary filled with familiar faces.

Michael and Karen met in 1994 and were married in 1996. Karen continued to work as a paralegal in a law office until early 2000 when she resigned to prepare for the radical change of becoming a mother. Michael switched employers in 1995 and again in late 1998. Thanks to his sharp increase in income, in early 1999 they purchased a new house in a new residential subdivision close to Michael's place of employment—and nine miles from the friends they had made back in that apartment building where they spent the first three years of their married life.

Since they were married back in 1996, Karen has left the full-time labor force to become a full-time homemaker, Michael has switched careers and employers, they have changed their place of residence, found a new church home, welcomed two babies, and created three new social networks—one based on Michael's friends at work, one built with new neighbors, and one consisting largely of parents of young children they have met at church. Emily spent two years meeting and making new friends earlier in the weekday pre-kindergarten at the church, and Jacob will soon enter into a similar career path. Three of Karen's closest friends and two of Michael's closest personal friends are parents they met in that program. Karen is a trustee at the church, and Michael is one of the seven lay elders. Those last three sentences help to explain why the Lancaster's friendship circle with fellow church members is the most cohesive and meaningful of the three.

While his new career does provide Michael with an excellent income, it requires him to be out-of-state three or four days in each of twenty weeks in the typical year. About ten times a year those trips bring him home late Saturday evening. One of the consequences is the family does not need a second income. Another is Karen carries most of the parenting responsibilities for those two children. A third is ten times a year that trip to church on Sunday morning reunites four people as they return to one of their favorite stability zones. As the Lancasters drive home after church, they travel from one stability zone to another stability zone.

The distinctive value of a stability zone is it provides continuity, predictability, and enduring relationships plus a comfortable and rarely changing physical environment. That continuity in the physical setting and the interpersonal relationships are mutually reinforcing. While the average worship attendance of about 125 makes that congregation the Lancasters attend a little too large to be an ideal stability zone, that limitation is partially offset by the fact that the minister who was the organizing mission developer in 1984 is now in his third decade as the pastor of this congregation.

Stability zones in Protestant congregations in contemporary America come in a huge variety of shapes and forms. One is sitting next to the same person in the same pew or chair in the same row during the corporate worship of God week after week. Another may be the extroverted personality who is the long tenured pastor. A third may be that adult Bible study group. A fourth may be the director of that chancel choir who excels in interpersonal skills and also can motivate the choir members to sing better than they know how to sing. A fifth may be the same parking space in that huge parking lot. A sixth may be the parish nurse who every week inquires, "How are you feeling today?" and expects at least a 40–300 word reply. A seventh may be the youth pastor who is identified by six dozen teenagers as "one of my four or five closest friends." An eighth may be that early Sunday morning worship service with thirty or forty in attendance that is offered "in the language I spoke for the first thirty-five years of my life before coming to America." A ninth may be that annual Christmas Eve or Good Friday worship service that uses the identical design year after year and decade after decade. A tenth may be that semi-retired pastor who now specializes as the minister of pastoral care. Thanks to the Internet, one of the fastest growing stability zones, which also resembles a great good third place, is the prayer cell consisting of five to a dozen women who live in several different states or countries, but who meet in a virtual community on the Web and pray for one another at least once a week. A twelfth was described to me by a person who is an active member of the three-year-old Monroe Street Fellowship averaging 35 at Sunday morning worship. It is one of sixty sites of this large multisite missionary church with a total combined weekend worship attendance of 2,200. Two people from that Monroe Street Fellowship now meet every Tuesday evening with a Bible study group at the central campus. The eleven single-parent mothers who constitute that group all identify this as an important stability zone and that room as a great good place.

The Third Place

Nineteen years following the publication of Toffler's book, another scholar came along and enriched our understanding of contemporary reality. Ray Oldenburg's thesis is that most adults in North America and Europe organize their life around three places. The first place is the home. A good home provides a healthy, supportive, and predictable environment for rearing children. The identity of the adults in the home often can be described by such words as wife, husband, mother, father, disciplinarian, breadwinner, parent, spouse, stepson, in-law, grandmother, or half-sister.

The second place in the lives of many adults and at least a million teenagers is where they work. Here one's identity often is described by job titles, expertise, professional competence, the work day, compensation, or duties.

The title of Oldenburg's book describes this third place as *The Great Good Place*. This third place is defined as "the core settings of informal public life . . . that host the regular, voluntary, informal, and happily anticipated gatherings of individuals beyond the realm of home and work."[4] The neighborhood tavern is one of Oldenburg's favorite examples of a good third place, but the number of neighborhood taverns has shrunk by at least 60 percent since 1960. That is a reflection of the fact that today's third place rarely can be identified in geographical terms. Fewer and fewer adults "neighbor" with people who reside nearby.

A good third place is where a person is identified by who you are as a person, not by what you do for a living or by your kinship ties. For some farmers in the early years of this century, it was a couple of hours in the blacksmith shop or in the hardware store on Saturday morning. For thousands of today's teenage boys the gang is their third place. For many choir members, the number-one third place in their life is the weeknight choir rehearsal. For others, it may be a bowling league or a service club or a softball team or a bridge club or a book group or a minor league baseball park. The Starbucks coffee shops have filled the need for a great good third place for a growing number of people in the twenty-first century.

The crucial distinctive characteristic of a good third place in today's world is that participants eagerly look forward to being with that same group of people in that familiar setting. It is increasingly difficult to identify the participants by the geo-

FROM COOPERATION TO COMPETITION

graphical proximity of their places of residence. That group of baseball fans who sit together in the same section of the bleachers may come from a twenty-mile radius.

For the workaholic, the place of work may be today's third place. For hundreds of "snowbirds," the winter residence on the west coast of Florida or in the valley in Arizona or Texas is their third place.

For millions of long-tenured church members, that congregation is their third place. They eagerly anticipate Sunday morning as a reunion with dear friends they have not seen for several days. This pattern is most clearly visible among some of the older adults in smaller congregations who now live alone and are not employed outside the home. For others, the third place is that adult Sunday school class they helped organize back in the midsixties. For many older women, the circle in the women's organization is a favorite third place. For a few, it is working in the church kitchen. For a growing number, it is that small Bible study-prayer group they helped start several years ago. In a growing number of congregations, the current third places include the mutual support groups created by the leaders of that parish. For some teenagers with few friends in school, their third place is the youth fellowship. For several young never-married adults, their favorite third place is working with friends on construction of a Habitat for Humanity® house. For many it is Wednesday night at church where the schedule begins with a meal and includes a dozen or more groups, meetings, and other gatherings. For a couple of dozen fathers, the new third place is that Saturday morning Bible study and prayer group they launched after attending a Promise Keepers weekend. The singles group that meets every Friday evening is the third place for many, most of whom are formerly married. For at least a few pastors, their third place is that Tuesday morning with a half-dozen other ministers organized around fellowship, coffee, candor, structured Bible study, sermon preparation, mutual support, and unneeded calories.

For some members, church is strictly a religious place. For others, it is primarily a great good third place in their lives. For many adults, church is a combination of spiritual nurture and a great good place.

The third part of this larger context takes the discussion down a side road to designing a strategy for initiating planned change from within an organization. What is the critical step in designing that strategy? When that question is directed at a half dozen experts on this subject, it is not unusual to receive nine or ten different answers. That list often includes (1) broaden the base of discontent with the status quo, (2) seek an inspiring leader who can articulate a vision of a new tomorrow that will win support on the basis of its merits, (3) build a supportive alliance of influential and respected leaders, (4) frame the proposal, not in terms of a choice between change and perpetuating the status quo, but in terms of a choice between Change A and Change B, (5) state the issue as a choice between desirable change and disaster, (6) create a sequence that gives every potential veto person time to talk themselves into supporting that new idea, (7) bring two or three of the potential influential opponents into the process early so the combination of time, learning, reflection, and the positive support of the proponents of change can transform them into supporters, (8) wait until a clear majority favors the proposed change before bringing it to a vote, (9) regard that first vote as a trial balloon, not a final decision, since many people cannot support any change until they have had at least one opportunity to reject it, and (10) check first to discover whether most of the people perceive this institution is now confronted with a crisis and therefore they are more likely to be receptive to proposals for radical change.

What Has That Larger Context Created?

If most of the people who will be affected by the proposed change do not see that congregation as their number-one stability zone or as their great good third place, but largely as the institutional expression of their faith as fully devoted followers of Jesus, change can be affirmed relatively easily. The key argument for the proposed change is this is necessary to enable this congregation to continue to be a faithful and obedient servant of God and to fulfill the Great Commission.

In real life the scenario may resemble this sequence. A group of seven volunteers from among the most loyal and deeply committed members of the congregation are asked to constitute a Long-Range Planning Committee. The first meeting is devoted to organizing and designing the process. The next several weekly meetings are devoted to Bible study in an effort to understand what God is calling that congregation to be and to be doing. They conclude the heart of the ministry consists of meaningful worship, the transformation of believers into fully devoted followers of Jesus and fulfilling the Great Commission.

Three or four months later they have prepared a three-part report. The first part articulates a vision of what this congregation should be seven years down the road. The second part describes the changes that must be made for today's congregation to match that vision of the future. The third part spells out in terms of six specific recommendations an implementation strategy. The threads connecting these parts lift up those three priorities of worship, the transformation of lives, and fulfilling the Great Commission. When the members of this committee present their report at a two-hour congregational meeting, they come prepared to defend it in terms of the centrality of worship, the focus on the transformation of believers into disciples, and the call to fulfill the Great Commission.

Most of the questions and objections they hear can be summarized in two sentences. This is not consistent with my definition of church as a stability zone! If this report is adopted and implemented, one consequence is this church no longer will meet my need for a meaningful third place!

That scenario helps to explain why proposals for change often generate conflict. That scenario also suggests that the potential impact on those treasured stability zones and this congregation as a great good place for many people should be considered in designing any strategy for helping a congregation to become competitive in the quest for future constituents. That scenario also raises the question of how can a strategy for

reaching younger generations be designed to strengthen existing stability zones rather than threatening them?

Eight Questions

*1. Why do so many Protestant congregations in America report an
average worship attendance between 18 and 40?* One reason is that
is about as many people as a great good third place can accommodate before anonymity and complexity begin to require
more structure than the participants can comfortably tolerate.

*2. Why do the vast majority of those congregations averaging fewer
than a hundred at worship tend to either remain on a plateau in size
or decline in numbers?* One reason is many already are too large.
The comfort level goes up as the proportion of people who are
"close personal friends of mine" increases and the proportion
who are acquaintances and strangers goes down.

*3. What have Michael, Karen, and their two children found in
their church that they value so highly?* It combines the best characteristics of a great good third place with the assets of a comfortable stability zone.

*4. Why are the vast majority of small and midsize congregations in
American Protestantism unable to initiate the changes required for
them to be able to reach, attract, serve, assimilate, nurture, disciple,
and challenge a larger number of people searching for a new church
home or who are on a personal religious quest?*

Because many of the current members prefer their congregation focus on strengthening its role as a stability zone and/or as
a great good place rather than attempting to attract a bunch of
strangers.

During the past eight years the membership at Faith Church
has decreased by 4 percent. A special Futures Committee is
appointed to design a strategy to reverse that trend. Ten months
later they produce a report that includes five recommendations
for reversing that numerical decline. Two that are at the heart
of that strategy require substantial changes. Two long-tenured
members oppose the first. Three of the most respected and
influential lay volunteer leaders oppose the second. One long-
tenured family is opposed to both.

In the small to midsize congregation every stability zone or great good place includes one or two members who are opposed to one or more of the proposed changes. Rather than disrupt their stability zone, other members agree "This needs more study" or "This is not the right time to make those changes" or "Let's not rock the boat now" or "I'm comfortable with the status quo."

In the large congregation averaging 700 at worship, the group life may include a total of 49 third places or face-to-face small groups. Those seven objectors are represented in five of the 49 face-to-face groups. Their influence is diluted. Most of the members of that congregation are either not aware of or are indifferent to their opposition.

What could have been a divisive conflict in the small church was avoided by taking no action to implement that recommended strategy. In the large congregation the recommended strategy was implemented and the price tag was the loss of four members, three of whom were virtual strangers to the majority of members. In the very large congregation anonymity can be both a problem and an asset.

5. It is not unusual to find a congregation that averaged 700 at worship one year increasing to 750 the following year. That required replacing approximately 50 people who left plus adding another 50 to produce that net increase of 50. That averaged out to a total gain of 100 new people, or 14 percent, to produce a net increase of 50 or 7 percent. If a large congregation can do that, why can't the congregation averaging 70 at worship add 10 new worshipers to produce a net increase of 5?

Among the many explanations for this pattern, these ten stand out as especially common. (1) That large congregation is organized to attract and assimilate newcomers while the smaller one is organized to take care of the current membership. (2) The leaders of that large congregation conceptualize it as a congregation of cells, choirs, circles, classes, stability zones, groups, third places, organizations, ministry task forces, and teams while the leaders in that smaller church tend to conceptualize it as a congregation of individuals, families, friendship circles, and committees. (3) Practice helps an institution move up the learning curve and every week that larger church practices how to attract, welcome, and assimilate new people. (4) That larger congregation is comfortable and competent functioning in a consumer-driven culture while the smaller church is more producer-driven: "This is what we offer, take it or go elsewhere." (5) That larger congregation is more likely to place a significant responsibility for continuity on long-tenured paid staff while the smaller church looks to committees, lay volunteers, real estate, the schedule, third places, stability zones, local traditions, the budget, and the denominational affiliation as sources of continuity. (6) That larger church concentrates on creating the new as part of a larger strategy for attracting and assimilating newcomers while the smaller congregation concentrates on perpetuating the old as an essential component of providing a comfortable stability zone for people. (7) The smaller congregation places a high value on a pastor who is a generalist, but also is highly competent in serving as a loving shepherd. The larger church places a high value on their senior minister being an excellent communicator of the gospel who also is a skilled team leader—the senior minister's weaknesses or areas of low competence are offset by paid specialists. (8) The criteria for congregational self-evaluation differ greatly; for example in that smaller congregation, two criteria for self-evaluation may be, "Is every member happy with what we're doing?" and "Are we able to pay all the bills on time?" While in the larger church those criteria may focus on the transformation of believers into disciples or expanding the range of choices offered people. (9) The small congregation counts the number of dollars sent away to hire someone else to do ministry while the large church counts the number of members who are engaged in doing ministry as short-term volunteers with fellow Christians in a sister church on another continent or as volunteers in sheltering the homeless or feeding the hungry or visiting people in prison. (10) The small church sends the pastor and/or volunteers to visit another church to learn how to do ministry in the twenty-first century while that larger congregation welcomes people who come there to learn how to do church in the twenty-first century.

6. *If congregational leaders, including the new pastor, decide to place a high priority on identifying and making the changes required for that church to become competitive in today's religious marketplace, what should they do first?* That is a difficult question! The answer must be customized to the local context. One option would be to identify the point of continuity in the life of that congregation that can be reinforced before introducing needed changes. Another option is to make changes by adding to the current schedule and ministry with close to zero subtractions. This is one argument in favor of becoming a multisite congregation rather than relocating the meeting place to a new site in order to have more space. Another option for the new pastor is to fulfill the responsibilities of the first round of earning the role of a respected and loving shepherd before moving into the role of the transformational leader. Affirm the value of stability zones while adding new choices for new people. Create one new "great good third place" every year. Identify at least one potential ally in every third place or stability zone if that is possible.

In summary, that customized ministry plan that is being implemented with highly desirable outcomes in a very large congregation probably cannot be adopted to fit the church that combines the characteristics of a comfortable stability zone with the value system of a great good third place.

7. *From a denominational perspective what is the impact of a denominational merger on the stability zones?* When a relatively small denomination merges with a very large denomination, the members of the smaller denomination may feel they have lost an important stability zone. This can be a crucial loss if that stability zone was reinforced by a strong ethnic or racial or ancestral heritage and/or a polity or belief system that is threatened by that merger. In the planning for that merger, what was done to help the smaller denomination compensate for the loss of their stability zone? If the answer is, "We didn't think about that," one consequence may be an unanticipated high number of departures by those who experienced that loss.

8. *In recent years several mainline Protestant denominations have adopted one or both of two major goals. One is to become more diverse in demographic terms.⁵ A second is to affirm an increase in theological or ideological pluralism.* This traveler's experience suggests the road to greater demographic diversity is relatively smooth if it is paved with a high level of agreement on such issues as doctrine, biblical interpretation, ideology, and polity.

The price tag on raising the level of theological or ideological pluralism within the denominational family is to increase the proportion of congregations in which nearly all members closely identify with two or more stability zones and/or view this parish as their "great good third place" and/or have their loyalty reinforced by the fact that several members of their personal social networks and/or their family tree are influential and respected volunteer leaders in that congregation. Those conditions usually are easy to meet in congregations averaging fewer than 40 or 50 at worship. They are much more difficult to fulfill in the congregations averaging 75–300 at worship.

The operational translation of those two paragraphs can be summarized in three sentences.

First, the goal is easier to attain if it focuses on either theological pluralism or demographic diversity. Demographic homogeneity can be the stability zone if the goal is theological pluralism. Likewise a clearly and precisely defined doctrinal position can be the stability zone if the goal is demographic diversity.

Second, if the goal is to achieve both demographic diversity and theological pluralism, the most practical strategy includes a strong affirmation of congregational autonomy, long pastorates, and relatively few congregations averaging more than 350 at worship.

Third, an alternative strategy for achieving both goals can include an affirmation of many small congregations, a high level of congregational autonomy, a decreasing number of congregations averaging 75–500 at worship, an increase in the number averaging over 1500 at worship, very long pastorates, and an acceptance of a diminishing total number of constituents and of continued disruptive intradenominational quarreling.

CHAPTER SEVEN

What Are the Safety Valves?

The competition among the churches in American Christianity for future constituents is becoming more intense. One consequence is millions of Christians have left the religious tradition in which they were reared to join one that speaks to them in terms of where they are on their personal religious pilgrimage. A second consequence is thousands of congregations operate on the assumption that they can be competitive by keeping on doing what they have always done, only doing it better. A third consequence is the decision in several religious traditions to proclaim God's truth in the same terms we have always proclaimed it and accept the fact that may produce shrinking numbers of constituents.

A fourth consequence is to assume that institutional loyalties will offset any internal conflict that may arise from either change or an unwillingness to change. That was a reasonably safe assumption in the 1950s, but not in the nineteenth century nor in the last four decades of the twentieth century. American church history in the nineteenth century is filled with descriptions of schisms. The past four or five decades alone have brought at least two dozen schisms, most of which were the by-products of denominational reunions and mergers.

The Frontier Response

One of the most widely used responses to discontent in American Protestantism has been for the discontented to depart and create a new denomination or association or federation or convention of congregations. (That response also has been implemented many times in Germany, Korea, and scores of other countries.)

The most significant response in American Christianity in recent decades has been the creation of Protestant megachurches. Several of these trace origins back to the 1940s and earlier, but the big national wave did not begin to appear until the 1960s. One explanation for the growth of this safety valve traces back to the growth of the American frontier. What could the residents of England, Scotland, Germany, Sweden, and a dozen other European countries do when they became discontented with the economy and culture into which they had been born and reared? One option was to immigrate to America. What could their descendants in New York, Pennsylvania, and Vermont do when they became disenchanted with the culture and the economy into which they had been born? Migrate to Ohio and Illinois was one option. What could the residents do when the Great Plains turned into a great dust bowl in the 1930s? Migrate to the West Coast.

What could the third generation German Reformed Church member do in the 1950s when that parent denomination decided to merge with the Congregational Christian Churches? Walk away and join another congregation in the Reformed tradition.

What could the "cradle Catholic" born in 1968 do when she became disenchanted with the limitations placed on women in the Roman Catholic Church in America? Walk away and join a Protestant congregation that combined an emphasis on liturgical worship with fewer restrictions on the role of women and the fringe benefit of inspirational sermons.

How Long Is the Agenda?

The 1960s brought a series of highly divisive items to the agendas in thousands of American Protestant congregations, theological schools, denominational systems, and church-related colleges. At or near the top of those agendas were the war in Vietnam, the future of the military draft, racism, ecumenism, *pelvic issues*, how much money congregations should collect and send to fund denominational budgets, the interpretation of Scripture, the role of women in the church, potential denominational mergers, divorce, the role of the laity, world missions, planting new missions versus financial subsidies for aging and numerically shrinking congregations, an expansion of the fringe benefits for the clergy, the future of tax-funded public schools in America, the role of the church in the inner city, the racial integration of white congregations, the beginning of the decline in the Sunday school, and the future of the traditional missionary organization for women born before 1920.

The guiding generalization is the longer the agenda, the more opportunities for people to choose up sides and quarrel.

One response to the intradenominational conflict generated by these and other disputes was to open the door to the organization of single issue lobbies, special interest groups, and caucuses. Some of these were funded by the denominational treasuries, but most were self-financing. When these were added to the existing system for making denominational decisions, the outcomes motivated a significant number of the laity to walk away in search of a religious system in which decisions were made "decently and in order."

In hundreds of congregations one consequence was to terminate their affiliation with that denomination. In others the "moderates" prevailed, and the compromise was to continue the denominational affiliation, but to reduce the number of dollars sent to fund denominational budgets.

Perhaps the most significant long-term consequence was represented by the millions of faithful churchgoers, both Catholic and Protestant, who simply walked away to worship with an independent or nondenominational megachurch. When asked why, a common explanation was, "Given a choice between a church in which the top priority was on intradenominational quarreling and one in which the top priorities were on the worship of God, transforming believers into disciples, and fulfilling the Great Commission, we chose the second."

A parallel explanation given by both laity and dozens of clergy reared in a denominationally affiliated congregation was relatively simple. "One way to avoid spending time and energy in intradenominational quarrels is to join a congregation that is not part of a denomination."

One reason it worked was the proliferation of parachurch agencies, teaching churches, retreat centers, and entrepreneurial individuals provided the resources that back in the 1950s congregations expected to receive from their denominational agencies. One consequence was greater competition for denominational agencies as they sought to provide the relevant resources needed by their affiliated congregations.

The Central Question

If you agree that competition is both a source and an outcome of change and that one by-product of change is conflict, what do you believe about that pattern of institutional behavior?

One suggestion discussed in the previous chapter is to perceive stability zones as potential allies in the process of initiating planned change from within an organization. That often requires thoughtful and precise wording of the issue.

A different strategy focuses on the nature and variety of safety valves that can reduce the pressure generated by changes in general and especially those that will produce substantial discontinuity with the past. While these do not represent an official position, the Southern Baptist Convention offers congregations at least seven different safety valves. One outcome is the Southern Baptist Convention has been among the most progressive in designing and implementing new ways of doing ministry in twenty-first-century America. Examples include a remarkable shift from being an almost all-white denomination in 1970 to a multicultural religious body in 2005, the creation of several models of the multisite option for congregations, substantial progress in changing from a regional religious body into a national denomination, challenging and equipping the laity to be engaged in doing ministry, the emergence of a large number of megachurches that display a high level of denominational loyalty, and continued growth in the combined worship attendance of all affiliated congregations on the typical weekend.

From this outsider's perspective seven of the most significant safety valves in the Southern Baptist Convention are these. Each one has reduced what otherwise could have been a temptation to engage in divisive and diversionary quarrels that would have undermined the call to fulfill the Great Commission.

1. Each congregation has the unilateral right to terminate its affiliation with the denomination but retain title to its assets. (This also is a significant safety valve in most but not all other Protestant denominations.)
2. In two states (Texas and Virginia), each with a very large and diverse constituency, congregations can choose the state convention with which they choose to affiliate.
3. Congregations determine how many dollars they will collect and send to help fund state and national budgets. Thus the floor does not become a ceiling.
4. While this is now under review, Southern Baptist congregations have long held the right to dual affiliation, to be full members of two different denominations.
5. While only six theological schools are partially funded by the national denominational budgets, students preparing for the parish ministry can choose from among several other Southern Baptist seminaries and divinity schools.
6. While this is not unique with the Southern Baptist Convention, and some would place it first on this list, every Southern Baptist member has the unilateral right to withdraw.

7. While the issue of control has come up and continues to be a divisive issue, the historic culture of that religious body supports the contention this religious body, including congregations, associations, state conventions, the Women's Missionary Union, and other national agencies, is organized around one unifying principle. That is to fulfill the Great Commission. This does NOT provide a fertile institutional context for intradenominational quarreling! Those readers who believe in the sinful nature of human beings, however, will understand that emphasis on evangelism and missions does not completely eliminate the temptation to quarrel over control.

Those seven safety valves will appear to be more valuable to readers who are affiliated with a congregation in which the polity traces back to Roman Catholic, Anglican, Reformed, or Methodist origins rather than to a free church or congregational system.

Finally, those readers who want to expand the list of C-words relevant to this discussion, such as competition, change, choices, and conflict, may want to add control to the list. Change and competition both encourage conflict over control.

CHAPTER EIGHT

What Are Useful Categories?

Hsow can human beings make sense out of this huge and complicated environment in which we exist? How can we help socialize our children into a culture that has changed so much since we were their age? How can we prepare for tomorrow when we know the future will bring challenges and opportunities that will differ greatly from those we faced yesterday?

One response is to divide our environment into categories and give a meaningful name to each category. This point is documented most clearly in Genesis 2:19. "God formed every animal of the field and every bird of the air . . . and whatever man called every living creature, that was its name."

The ritual for infant baptism in several Christian bodies includes the question directed to the parents, "By what name shall this child be called?"

We give a different name to each day of the week. When we wake up in the morning, many of us ask ourselves, "What day is this? What opportunities and obligations will this day bring?"

One of the most widely used systems for making order out of complexity on this planet has been to divide the population into a half dozen categories. In the English language the traditional labels placed on these categories have been families, clans, tribes, coalitions, nations, and strangers. Strangers often are identified as foreigners or aliens or invaders or enemies. After two centuries of fighting wars against enemies identified as nations, in September 2001 the United States found itself engaged in combat with enemies that resembled clans and tribes rather than nations.[1]

A simpler way to divide the world into categories is "us" and "them." This is a widely used system among contemporary street gangs, by the United States military forces in Iraq, by Protestants who relied on anti-Catholicism as a basic unifying principle in the 1840–1965 era, by the abolitionist movement in the nineteenth century, by the Ku Klux Klan, by the Anti-Saloon League, by both sides in heresy trials, by both candidates in the presidential campaign of 2004, and by those choosing up sides in the intradenominational quarrels within several mainline Protestant denominations in recent years. The smaller the number of categories, the easier it is to choose up sides! The larger the number of categories, the greater the need to create coalitions and alliances.

In the ideal world everything can be divided into two categories. Squirrels, for example, divide acorns into two categories. Those that are most perishable, such as the acorns from white oak trees, should be eaten as soon as possible. By contrast, acorns from red oaks are the least perishable. Therefore they can be buried to be eaten during the winter.

When state legislatures redistrict congressional seats following each decennial census, a common practice is to maximize the number of "safe" seats and minimize the number that probably will be closely contested.

That introduces another characteristic of this process of dividing the world into relatively homogeneous categories. To reduce what otherwise would be confusion, words are used to describe these lines of demarcation. One set of these names is used to describe opposite values or categories. These pairs include good or bad, friend or foe, high or low, rich or poor, strong or weak, healthy or sick, young or old, believer or nonbeliever, ordained or lay, north or south, and winner or loser.

The specific category in which we place ourselves often influences how we will respond when a particular subject is being discussed. An ancient illustration is when the subject of death is raised. The young person responds, "Who? Me?" The middle-aged adult asks, "When?" The elderly wonder, "How?"

The veteran teacher goes away for a three-day continuing education experience. Upon entering into that experience the adult accepts the role of learner rather than last week's role as teacher.

If the issue is a request for $100 from each person, one category of people will respond, "Sure!" while another group will declare, "That's too much!" A couple of hours later one of those who objected to a request for $100 purchases a new suit for $300 and considers that to be an exceptional bargain. The environmental setting carries a name and that name becomes the basis for deciding whether $100 represents a lot of money or is a bargain. The category in which we place ourselves tells us how to respond.

What Is the Reference Point?

Unless the categories are clearly and precisely defined, their use often becomes a source of confusion. One example of this surfaced in the election campaigns of 2004. A number of pundits and journalists used a category named "The Religious Right" to describe one slice of the electorate. This usually was interpreted as a reference to adult Christians in the United States who were both theologically conservative in terms of their interpretation of Scripture and also conservative in a variety of political, social, and economic issues. It was widely assumed that the vast majority of "The Religious Right" would vote for George W. Bush in November.

The exit polls in November 2004, however, suggested that millions of Americans who are clearly on the conservative side of the theological spectrum cast their votes for John F. Kerry. They included an overwhelming majority of black Protestant Christians as well as a large number of working-class Catholics, low-income whites who trace their ancestry back to western

Europe, and recent immigrants from Latin America. One reason John Kerry failed to win the 2004 election is he did not make an effective appeal to those voters who are theologically conservative and politically liberal.

Another example of the use of categories to oversimplify a complex issue is the use of tax-funded vouchers to enable parents to enroll their children in the school of their choice. It is widely assumed this is an issue favored by conservatives and opposed by liberals. In a recent poll conducted by the Gallup organization for Phi Delta Kappa, 54 percent of the national sample of adults opposed vouchers while only 42 percent supported them, and 4 percent chose the "Don't Know" response. When that part of the sample consisting of parents with public school age children was asked which type of school they would choose if given a full tuition voucher, 38 percent chose a public school, 40 percent preferred a church-related private school, and 17 percent picked a non-church-related private school while 5 percent checked the "Don't Know" option.

Several polls in this same series conducted in earlier years revealed a substantial majority of black parents with school age children expressed a strong preference for tax-funded vouchers that would enable them to enroll their children in the school of their choice.

The 2004 poll reported that 43 percent of the parents of public school students were "more likely" to support a candidate for national office who supported vouchers for private schools while 36 were "less likely" to support such a candidate.[2]

In other words, race or marital status are more useful categories than "liberal" or "conservative" in predicting how Americans will respond to the issue of offering parents a tax-funded choice in picking a school for their children.

How Do You Classify Congregations?

For most of the past three centuries of American church history a dozen sets of categories have dominated the processes for classifying religious congregations. One, which is still widely used, is the ancestry of the members. Words such as Dutch,

German, Swedish, Colored, Polish, Italian, Negro, Japanese, Black, Slovak, Chinese, Scotch, Latino, African American, Korean, Afro-Centric, and Cuban have been and continue to be used for classifying Christian congregations in the United States.

A second goes back into the early nineteenth century and was popularized by Will Herberg in his book, *Protestant, Catholic, Jew*.[3] That system reflected the dominant role of those three religious traditions.

A third system that continues to be widely used in the yellow pages in the telephone directories, in the self-identification efforts of a shrinking proportion of Protestant congregations, in gatherings of representatives from several religious traditions, in a shrinking number of advertisements by congregations in local newspapers, and by a decreasing number of adults enrolling in a theological seminary peaked in popularity in the early decades of the twentieth century. This system called for classifying Protestant congregations by their denominational affiliation. This system, however, appears to be of diminishing influence among adults born after 1960 who are searching for a church home. They are more likely to be heavily influenced by the relevance and quality of the ministries than by the denominational label.

Back in the 1950s a fourth and widely used line of demarcation in American Protestantism for classifying both parish pastors and congregations was based on the location of the meeting place and divided the universe into two categories. One was described by the word "rural," the other by the word "urban." In most denominations the rural church and the rural ministers outnumbered their urban counterparts, but the urban congregations included more people.

A widely shared assumption was the appropriate preparation for serving an urban congregation began with college, followed by seminary, followed by one or two relatively brief pastorates in one or two or three rural churches. One explanation for that sequence was it sorted out those who had a genuine and deep commitment to the parish ministry from those who were called to be scholars. A more influential factor may have been the salary schedule was more attractive in the urban churches.

Demographic changes led to an explanation of that rural-urban (or rural-city in a few traditions) division into a three-part classification of rural, suburban, and city with that third group reserved for congregations gathering for worship in a building in the central city. By the early 1960s the migration of tens of thousands of Americans from a rural residence into the central city plus the exodus of upper- and upper-middle-class whites to suburbia led a few observers to suggest the denominational specialists in ministries with rural people should focus their efforts on the older sections of the large central cities while the experts on the city church should work with suburban congregations.

While it was frowned on by egalitarians and often represented an excessively simplistic definition of reality, a fifth system based on occupation and social class has been widely used to classify churches in America. Old First Church Downtown often was described as "where the shakers and movers go to church" while thousands of other congregations were identified as "a farming community church" or "a mining town church" or as "the college church" or as the congregation for employees of a large factory.

The last half of the twentieth century introduced a sixth conceptual framework for the classification of both the clergy and congregations. This was based on a slowly growing conviction that average worship attendance was a more sensitive yardstick than membership to measure the size of a Protestant church in America. It also was a more accurate indicator of numerical growth versus numerical decline. It was not unusual to find a congregation reporting an increase in membership year after year after year while the average worship attendance continued to decrease.

As more and more denominations added a column for average worship attendance to the annual report form to be completed by each affiliated congregation, this became a useful line of demarcation in classifying churches. (By 1965 this observer had become convinced it was the most useful single statistical criterion for classifying congregations.)

The combination of the growth of the ecumenical movement after World War II plus the dominant role in American Protestantism of what at the time were approximately two dozen denominations (since reduced to about ten as a result of mergers) produced a seventh line of demarcation. This placed the "cooperative" denominations on one side of that line and the "non-cooperative" on the other side. That system for classifying congregations began to disappear in the 1960s with the numerical expansion of several newer religious traditions plus the arrival on the American ecclesiastical landscape of that rapidly growing number of nondenominational or independent churches.

The successor for that system was an eighth line of demarcation. On one side were the congregations affiliated with a "Mainline Protestant denomination" while the opposite side was reserved for "Other."

The religious revival that began in the 1960s called for a new system. One response was to turn to a theological spectrum. At one end were the congregations identified as "Fundamentalist." Next to them were the "Conservatives." At the opposite end were the "Liberals" and the "Progressives." Scattered across the middle of this ninth spectrum were (a) congregations that did not want to replay a popular game of the 1920s, (b) congregations that preferred to focus on fulfilling the Great Commission, and (c) congregations that chose to focus on other internal questions.

Perhaps the number-one outcome of the use of this system for classifying congregations was it made it easier for Southern Baptists, United Methodists, Presbyterians, Episcopalians, and others to choose up sides in a new indoor game called "Intradenominational Quarreling."

Two Other Categories

At this point a few readers may raise this question, "Why have the numbers of dollars sent to fund denominational budgets and causes not been mentioned?"

That is a fair question. In several Protestant denominations, one of the most widely used categories for evaluating congregational performance is the monthly or quarterly or annual report by the treasurer of each regional judicatory. In several cases that report includes four vertical columns—the name of the congregation, the amount of money requested, the amount received to date at denominational headquarters, and the percentage paid on that requested amount.

The influence of this criterion for evaluating congregational performance can be reinforced by giving awards to congregations that meet or exceed their quota and/or to those that have increased the proportion paid by the largest percentage and/or to those that contribute the most on a per member basis.

(The point here is not to challenge the need to fund denominational budgets. Those dollars are needed! Experience suggests that asking congregations to collect those dollars and forward them to denominational headquarters began to become an obsolete strategy in the 1960s. If the goal is to raise more than $30 annually per member for regional and national denominational budgets, there are more effective methods for achieving that goal. One relevant generalization is that goal is more easily attainable in those denominations in which the top priority is on fulfilling the Great Commission. It is more difficult to reach that goal if the denominational culture is designed to encourage intradenominational quarreling. It also is easier to reach that goal if the average worship attendance for the denomination has been rising rather than dropping. It is easier to achieve a goal that averages out to more than $30 per member if the vast majority of those dollars go directly to designated causes and if the donors receive an accurate annual accounting of the ministry goals that were achieved.)

Under the broader umbrella of the redistribution of income is an eleventh category. This is the annual report on the direct financial subsidy received during the past year by each congregation or mission or cause that is subsidized by that denominational system. This is less useful today than in former times as more and more congregations are relying on indirect financial subsidies that rarely are reported. Examples include the ministerial placement process, the cost of providing staff services to congregations, financing health benefits for retired ministers, the cost of denominationally sponsored continuing education experiences, or the cost of holding denominational meetings and conventions.

The reason they have been ignored in this chapter is the theme. Which are the most useful categories for classifying congregations if the goal is to help facilitate change and to be able to compete with other churches for future constituents in the years ahead? Long-term financial subsidies, either direct or indirect, can be useful if the goal is either perpetuating the past or simply institutional survival. Likewise we have no persuasive evidence that demonstrates helping to finance denominational budgets is a source of vitality for congregational life nor a productive strategy for enabling the donor congregation to become more competitive in the religious marketplace.

Administrative Convenience

Finally we come to the last of this list of a dozen traditional systems for classifying congregations in American Christianity. It also is the most widely used system today. Its origins date back to when a horse was the fastest means of transportation in America. This system classifies congregations by the post office that represents the address for each congregation. Congregations located in the same geographical area are assigned to the same regional judicatory for administrative purposes. The names of these administrative units vary and include words such as synod, conference, diocese, district, classes, presbytery, association, convention, and region. The primary motivations for utilizing this system obviously were administrative convenience and travel. One consequence is that in the twenty-first century a Presbyterian congregation may be in one presbytery for administrative purposes, but concurrently be a member of a local interfaith alliance focused on social justice issues while concurrently an active participant in a national network of very large churches and a partner in a regional coalition of churches representing one caucus at national denominational meetings.

This system also may mean that a congregation with its meeting place in northern Virginia should be affiliated with the Virginia regional judicatory of that denomination, even if one-half or more of the members work and/or reside in the District of Columbia.

This system for classifying congregations also illustrates how the lines of demarcation and the words attached to describe each subgroup influence policy-formulation, decision-making, and the responsibilities of the professional staff. For example, in the United Methodist Church at least two hundred district superintendents need to master a variety of skills ranging from personnel decisions to reversing the numerical decline of a downtown church to helping an open country rural congregation make the transition from serving farmers to building ministries with employees in the recreational industry to raising money from a dozen supportive wealthy donors to plant a new mission to counseling an ex–neighborhood church on how to become a large regional congregation to career counseling for pastors who need to find a new vocation to encouraging a large congregation to accept a new role as a multisite church to staffing a campus ministry.

One alternative is to replace that old classification system based on the geographical location of the meeting place with a new system based on points of commonality in ministry. In simple terms, move from geography to affinity in designing the categories to be used in classifying congregations.[4]

This chapter affirms the value of categories for classifying congregations. The number-one reason for using an affinity system of classification is to facilitate peer learning. Rather than hope the congregation averaging 935 at worship will be inspired and mentored on improved ways to do ministry in the twenty-first century by visiting three different nearby congregations, each averaging 30–40 at worship, the assumption is the seven-year-old new mission can learn by visiting another seven-year-old new mission or one multisite congregation can learn by visiting another multisite church even if the meeting places are separated by a four hour drive.

Likewise this chapter is based on the assumption that a classification system can be devised that will reflect the characteristics of those congregations most likely to be able to compete for potential future constituents in the years ahead. This next collection of a dozen categories also can be utilized by congregational leaders who are identifying the changes that will be needed for their church to be competitive in the twenty-first century. Equally important, these categories can be used in identifying those congregations "that are similar to our church and from whom we can learn how we can create a more effective ministry here in our community."

Finally, this optimist believes from personal experiences that a customized combination of categories can enable denominational policy-makers to fulfill their dream that "the best days in the history of our denomination are ahead of us." Instead of classifying congregations by the location of their meeting place or the community setting or by the credentials earned by the current pastor or the compensation they provide for their minister, classify them by affinity and/or by their capability to be competitive in the twenty-first century.

Asking a Better Question

If we shift the focus of this discussion from one narrow slice of American church history or from how to choose up sides for intradenominational quarrels, back to the central theme of this book, it is necessary to rephrase the question. Instead of asking, "How do you classify churches in American Protestantism?" we need to recognize that the wording of the question influences the responses. That point was illustrated by the earlier discussion of how people respond when polled about parental choice and vouchers. The term "voucher" tends to evoke negative responses while "parental choice" is more likely to evoke positive answers.

A more relevant question for this book is, "What are the most useful categories for classifying congregations if the goal is to help them respond creatively and positively to a changing context for ministry and to a rise in the level of competition for people's time, commitment, energy, loyalty, and money?"

The critics, of course, will object that is an admission that Americans now live in a consumer-driven culture and recognition of that trend gives it legitimacy. Affirming consumerism as a fact of contemporary American life does carry an implied affirmation of the fact that Lutheran parishes now compete with Presbyterian, Episcopalian, Baptist, Methodist, and non-denominational congregations for future constituents. The critics may respond that if competition is a fact today, it should be deplored and corrected, not accepted as a factor in designing a ministry plan for the early years of the twenty-first century.

The bias in this book is that effective planning for tomorrow must be based, to the fullest extent possible, on a realistic definition of contemporary reality, rather than on a dream of how the religious scene in America should be today and tomorrow. A completely neutral or value-free ideological environment does not exist!

Another bias in this book is the leader with a system that is consistent with contemporary reality possesses a huge advantage over the leader who uses a system based on an obsolete definition of contemporary reality or the person who does not have a system. The big flaw in that long sentence is it overlooks a common barrier to change. That barrier is the leader who is reasonably comfortable in denial. One expression of denial is, "I'm comfortable with the system we now use to classify our congregations." Another is a refusal to admit this congregation or this denominational system no longer is competitive. A third is to defend an obsolete system and concentrate on identifying the obvious scapegoats who have failed to make that system produce the desired outcomes.

One response to denial is to look at the merits of other systems. Here are a dozen different systems with a brief discussion of the merits of each. The twelfth most useful is described followed by the eleventh, tenth, ninth, and on to the second. This ranking is based on how useful this traveler has found them to be in helping congregations design a customized ministry plan in a rapidly changing cultural, social, and economic context while faced with an increasing level of competition for future constituents. Unfortunately the most useful is the most subjective to measure and difficult to define.

XII. What Drives the Planning Process?

This system is placed last among these twelve, not because of a low value, but rather because it is (a) difficult to persuade leaders to use and (b) rarely utilized. In the ideal world it would be among the three most valuable systems for classifying congregations.

For this discussion we can condense the number of subgroups to a dozen of the most widely used in contemporary American Protestantism. The critical issue is to select the approach that will encourage receptivity to change and that is compatible with becoming competitive in the religious marketplace.

1. The perception of a scarcity of resources. The participants plan on the assumption they are limited by a scarcity of volunteers, money, space, potential future constituents, time, creativity, or energy. That encourages a rationing approach and places a low ceiling on what is possible.
2. Tradition. How we did it last year becomes the driving precedent for how we will do it tomorrow. That discourages change.
3. A demand for participatory democracy. The voice and vote of each member should carry the same weight as that of any other member. The uninformed opinion is given as much weight as the well-informed opinion. The exceptionally articulate opponent may be more influential than the most fully informed advocate of change. This often produces a search for a consensus. One way to achieve that is to accept compromises that represent the lowest common denominator.

4. The vision, goals, and competence of the founding pastor. In new missions this often produces a congregation that plateaus in size with an average worship attendance under 40. If that mission developer pastor combines the gift of visionary leadership with the ability to enlist allies with an exceptionally high level of competence as a communicator of the gospel of Jesus Christ plus an attractive personality, this approach may produce a congregation averaging more than 500 one year after that first public worship service.

5. The board of elders. This often is a comfortable alternative for the congregation averaging 60–135 at worship if the members are comfortable with the status quo. Asking the current governing board to add to their list of responsibilities the responsibility for (a) designing a ministry plan for the next five to seven years plus (b) a strategy for implementing it, has two limitations. First, it probably means overloading busy people. Second, the criteria for choosing the members of a long-range planning task force may overlap the criteria for selecting elders, but they are far from identical!

6. A priority to take better care of today's members. This is a common pattern today in the numerically shrinking and aging congregation founded before 1960.

7. A passion to fulfill the Great Commission. This usually requires an exceptionally high level of competent visionary leadership, a readiness to design a customized ministry plan that matches discretionary resources with a realistic and precise definition of the characteristics of the people to be reached and a strategy that is relevant to their needs.

8. A passion to organize the ministries of this congregation in obedience to Matthew 25:34-43. For those congregations that (a) represent a high degree of demographic diversity as well as an unusually broad range of theological pluralism and/or (b) have limited resources, this often requires a decision-making process that minimizes internal conflict in the ranking of priorities.

9. An intentional delegation of the responsibility and authority to design a customized ministry plan to one of two groups. One is the paid program staff plus two or three widely respected and influential lay volunteers. This is a common model in congregations averaging more than 500 at worship.

An alternative is the ad hoc Long-Range Planning Committee. This often includes the pastor, perhaps one other paid staff member, two or three future-oriented lay volunteers plus two widely respected and influential laypersons who help give credibility to the recommendations of this group.

10. Fulfilling denominational goals. While less common today than in 1955, this model is used in denominationally affiliated congregations in which the pastor and at least a dozen members place a high priority on helping to fulfill denominational goals. The crucial issue is whether the resulting strategy is consistent with enabling that congregation to be competitive with other churches in attracting future constituents.

11. The support and approval of one or two or three key families. This is a widely used model in thousands of small Protestant congregations.

12. "Act your size!" One of the most effective strategies for reducing the size of the congregation that has increased from an average worship attendance of 120 a decade ago to 185 today is act and plan like a congregation averaging 125 at worship.

A more useful expression of this approach is, "Act the size that is appropriate for the role you believe God has called this congregation to accept and fulfill in the years ahead."

Which of these twelve is the appropriate choice for your congregation?

XI. The Community Context?

For at least eighty years this has ranked at or near the top of the list of the most widely used components of a larger system for helping congregations design a customized ministry plan.

Several decades ago while working as a city planner, I was taught that preparing a comprehensive analysis of the community context constituted at least two-thirds of the work required to prepare a master plan for the future use of land and money in a city. That analysis included demographic trends, past and current land use patterns, transportation needs, economic and employment data, anticipated capital improvements, probable future expenditures and receipts, and the current political realities.

A parallel analysis for congregational planning could produce a forty-page document. For this discussion, however, the central variables in the community context can be summarized in five generalizations.

1. The more rapid the rate of the increase in the population, the higher the level of competition among the churches for future constituents. In this scenario a rising tide usually sinks several ships in that harbor.
2. The larger the number (number, not proportion) of residents who own their homes, the more intense that competition.
3. A rise in the social class status of the residents usually is matched by an increase in the competition among the churches for future constituents.
4. An increase in the number of Protestant congregations that have been worshiping in the same building at the same address for fewer than ten years usually creates an increase in the level of competition among the churches for future constituents.
5. Since multiethnic congregations continue to be a rarity in American Protestantism, substantial changes in the ethnic, language, national ancestry, skin color, or social class of the population usually call for substantial changes from the past in designing a congregation's ministry plan for the future!

X. How Long at This Address?

The most influential memories for most of us began following a point of discontinuity in our life. "When we moved here,

FROM COOPERATION TO COMPETITION

my life took a new turn." "After I finished high school, I . . ." "After we were married . . ." "When our first child was born, my life changed." "Following our divorce . . ." "When, at age twenty-seven, I accepted Jesus Christ as my Lord and Savior . . ." "After I returned from military service . . ." "When my husband died . . ." "When I switched jobs, my life . . ." "When our house was destroyed in Hurricane Katrina . . ." "Our church began to go downhill when Reverend Harrison retired and it still hasn't recovered." "My wife and I joined this congregation about a year before we relocated and built the new church on this new site and . . . ." "It's nearly four years since my husband retired, and he still hasn't figured out how to keep busy."

The more years that separate that point of discontinuity from today, the larger the package of memories we have accumulated since that date. The longer a congregation has been gathering together in that same room for the corporate worship of God, the larger the quantity of sacred memories that are stored in that room. The longer a congregation has been worshiping at the same address, the greater the resistance to change.

Faith Church was organized in 1908. The newly constructed building completed in 1925 on what was an adequate site at a central location has evolved into a functionally obsolete structure on an inadequate site with only seven offstreet parking spaces at what has become a poor location. Only two of the current members were even alive when this building was constructed to replace the old white frame church four blocks to the west that had been destroyed by fire in 1924. If this congregation could relocate after only sixteen years in that building, why can't we relocate and construct new facilities on a larger site with plenty of offstreet parking at a more highly visible and more accessible location?

Why not relocate? One reason is the number of years between 1925 and today is more than five times sixteen! That relocation of 1925 (a) was forced by a fire and (b) encountered only one-fifth the resistance a proposal to relocate might encounter today. That fire created two options—build on this site or relocate and build at a new location. The fire eliminated maintaining the status quo as an option. The choice in 1924 was between Change A and Change B. Back in 1924 the members probably needed only a few weeks to talk themselves into choosing Change B over Change A. When the choice is between continuity with the past and discontinuity, most people naturally will choose continuity with the past if that appears to be a possible alternative. The greater the perceived gap between continuity and discontinuity, the longer the time period required by normal human beings to talk themselves into supporting discontinuity.

Why classify congregations by how long they have been gathering to worship God at the same address? Six reasons. First, if that time period is in excess of two or three decades, any proposal that represents substantial discontinuity with the past is unlikely to win immediate approval. Second, do not mistake initial resistance for unreserved opposition. What often is perceived as early opposition to change may be simply a preference for continuity. Third, give people adequate time to talk themselves into supporting a new idea. If a vote is called for prematurely, those "No" votes may really mean, "We haven't had sufficient time to persuade ourselves we favor change. If you insist on a premature decision, we have no choice but to oppose this new idea." In other words, a "No" response may in fact mean, "Not yet."

Fourth, the longer the congregation has been meeting at the same address, the more likely the road to ultimate approval requires a rest stop at a time and place where that proposal for change can first be rejected. Thus when that proposed change calling for meaningful discontinuity with the past is rejected, how do the advocates for change interpret that negative response? They ask themselves several questions. Did we push for a premature decision? If so, what must we do before we bring it up again? How much time should we allow before calling for a new vote? Would it be wise to rephrase the question? Instead of asking people to vote "Yes" or "No" on a proposal for change, can we restate it as a choice between Option A and Option B? For example, a proposal to relocate the meeting place could be stated as a choice between growing older in the age of our members and adjusting to a decline in numbers versus relocating to a site where we can reach, attract, and serve younger generations.

Fifth, a crisis changes the rules. A more precise statement is the widespread perception of a crisis changes the rules. One example of that came on December 7, 1941. A second example came six decades later on September 11, 2001. It is not irrelevant to note that this nation's elected leader, President Franklin D. Roosevelt, gave one of his greatest speeches in December 1941. He described the crisis, identified the probable implications, and rallied the people in support of the cause. President George W. Bush did the same in September 2001. When your congregation or denomination is confronted with a crisis, who will articulate a relevant challenge?

Finally, denial is the most common response to a pattern that reveals an institution is drifting from a competitive position into irrelevance and obsolescence. The greater the attachment to the past, the more fertile the climate for denial. Moving out of denial often is the first essential step in initiating planned change from within an organization. One path out of denial is the crisis created by external forces. Another road out of denial calls for flooding the system with information and giving people time to digest that new information before asking them to pay the price of discontinuity with the past in exchange for a new tomorrow. An overlapping strategy states the issue as a choice between Change A and Change B.

IX. What Is the Tenure of Today's Members?

The length of time a congregation has been meeting at the same address is one way to determine the content of the institutional memory. An overlapping, but different approach to classifying congregations is by the tenure of today's members and especially of the lay volunteers who are influential policy-makers. The longer the tenure of the members in general and especially of these volunteer policy-makers, the more likely proposals for change that will produce great discontinuity with the past will encounter substantial resistance. A common example is the proposal to revise the Sunday morning schedule from Sunday school followed by worship to early worship followed by Sunday school followed by a late worship service. If that has been the schedule for a couple of decades or more and most of the current volunteer leaders joined before 1990, that proposed change probably will encounter more resistance than if three-fourths of today's adult members joined in 2004 or later.

One compromise is to avoid changing the status quo on Sunday morning and suggest change by addition. Avoid creating losers who will have to change their schedule on Sunday morning. Expand the weekend worship schedule by adding a Saturday evening service.

VIII. How Open to Technology?

During the past seventy-five years changes driven by modern technology have revolutionized agriculture, mining, manufacturing, the practice of medicine, retail trade, communications, transportation, education, entertainment, recreation, the relationships of a person's place of residence to that individual's place of work, and many other facets of life.

The institutional expression of any fellowship that affirms the value of interpersonal relationships naturally tends to be resistance to changes that will create greater discontinuity with the past. The larger the number of living adults in that religious body and/or the longer that religious body has been in existence in the United States, the more likely the current leadership will resist change. The smaller the size of the congregation and/or the larger the proportion of congregations that average fewer than 40 at worship and/or the longer back in history that congregation or denomination traces its origins, the more likely the road to obsolescence will be more attractive than the road to relevance in the twenty-first century.

One consequence is those denominational systems in America that came into existence after 1900 are more likely to be attracting Americans born after 1965 than are the systems that trace their origins back to the seventeenth or eighteenth centuries. A more highly visible example is the congregations founded after 1980 are more likely to utilize the power of projected visual imagery in worship than are the congregations organized before 1980.

For most of American church history the vast majority of Christians walked to church. That reinforced the conviction that congregations should design their ministry plans to reach and serve families who lived within a two or three mile radius of the meeting place. The number of registered automobiles in the United States increased from 8.1 million in 1920 to 40.3 million in 1950 to 75.3 million in 1965. Despite the impact of that technological change, in 1965 many of the experts in urban ministries were urging congregational leaders to focus on "serving the people in your neighborhood." During the past half century technologically driven change has eliminated the family doctor who housed his practice in his home, the neighborhood grocery store, the neighborhood post office, the neighborhood tavern, the neighborhood motion picture theater, the village high school, and the hardware store on Main Street. By 2005, when the number of registered motor vehicles designed for personal or family use exceeded 165 million, it was becoming clear that the small neighborhood congregation could not compete in attracting younger generations with the large regional church with a clearly defined role and ministry.

Technology also has helped to transform the old emphasis from teaching into a new focus on learning, to create a national ministerial marketplace for congregations seeking a successor for that recently departed pastor, to replace the advertisement on the religion page of the local newspaper with an interactive Web site, to supplement the residence-based theological school with a distance learning curriculum, and to be in regular real time interactive communication with "the missionary couple we help support in Africa."

One reason to include this as a useful category for classifying congregations, and denominations, should be obvious. This can be helpful in identifying those congregations that are most likely to be willing to make the changes required to be competitive.

VII. Tomorrow's New Constituents?

"Who are the people beyond our current membership that we are seeking to reach, attract, serve, nurture, assimilate, and challenge in the near future?" This description of potential future constituents is a widely used concept in contemporary American Protestantism. One response is, "Everyone!" That makes it impossible to agree on priorities since no one congregation can mobilize the resources required to fulfill that dream.

The variety of other responses can be illustrated by a dozen examples:

1. The children of today's membership. The top priority is to retain our own people and their offspring.
2. Nonmembers who marry a member. Instead of following the old American tradition that the bride adopts her husband's religious affiliation, the goal is to make marriage a major entry point for future members. This was a major goal in most Roman Catholic parishes in America up through the mid-1960s.
3. People who recently came to the United States from the same country that was the place of birth for most of our adult members.
4. Skin color. People with a white skin go to white churches. People with a black skin go to black churches. This continues to be a widely used system for identifying potential future constituents. The rapid increase in the number of black-white marriages has begun to undermine the use of this line of demarcation.
5. We focus on nonbelievers and our number-one evangelistic priority is to convert nonbelievers to the Christian faith.
6. Ditto except the focus is on adherents to another religious belief system.
7. Our number-one goal is to transform self-identified Christians who display a low commitment to Jesus Christ as Savior into fully devoted apostles of Jesus Christ.

8. Our number-one outreach is to attract church shoppers who are new residents in this community or self-identified Christians with no active church affiliation who have begun a new religious quest.
9. Our number-one goal is a product of the fact our members are growing old. Therefore our top priority is to attract people in the 20–40 age bracket, both single and married.
10. Our slogan is, "We are here to help you rear your children." Our ministry is designed to attract parents who want help in rearing their children in an avowedly Christian culture that transmits Christian values to their children. A tuition-funded Christian day school often is the center piece of a large package of these ministries.
11. We have created a new ministry for mothers who have just given birth. This is designed to help mothers learn how to enrich the process of early childhood development with music. Research on the brain has demonstrated that music is a natural channel of communication for infants. This ministry is staffed by a team led by a grandmother who has had specialized training in the role of music in early childhood development.
12. Our primary focus in our evangelistic outreach is to welcome adults who have become discontented with the doctrinal stance of the congregation and/or religious body with which they have been affiliated and are searching for a church in which the preaching and teaching match their belief system.

This focus on potential future constituents has become a popular, but relatively unsophisticated, system for classifying congregations. To be useful it must be refined and expanded. That point can be illustrated by asking a half-dozen questions.

First, is the focus on classifying people by their age and marital status or the life cycle (examples 1, 2, 9, 10, and 11) or by stages of a personal faith journey (examples 5, 6, 7, and 12) or by ancestry (examples 3 and 4) or on those who take the initiative to come to our church (examples 8 and maybe 12)? Or is the focus really on people who fit into two or three of those groups? Or is this really a wish, not a precisely defined constituency?

For example, that young adult, age 20–40, category includes residents of the United States who are (1) married couples with young children at home, a husband who works full time and a wife who is a full-time homemaker, (2) a never-married twenty-two-year-old gang member, (3) a recently widowed mother of two who is the beneficiary of a $1 million life insurance policy, (4) a homeless alcoholic thirty-seven-year-old male, (5) a female university professor married to a male university professor, (6) a single never-married disabled veteran of the war in Iraq, (7) a black twenty-nine-year-old recent immigrant from Nigeria, (8) a thirty-four-year-old physician who came to the United States after graduation from medical school in India, (9) a never-married thirty-seven-year-old grandmother of four, (10) a twenty-year-old college student with wealthy parents, (11) a migrant from Mexico working in construction to send money back home to Mexico, and (12) a divorced mother of three who is heavily dependent on public assistance for an income. What is the strategy that will enable the congregation averaging 125 at worship to reach and serve all of those young adults?

Second, what are the needs of the people we are seeking to reach and attract? What will be the components of an effective strategy to reach and serve that constituency?

Third, what resources will we need to mobilize to be able to implement that strategy?

Fourth, what changes in our schedule, staffing, real estate, public image, finances, and priorities will we need to make to be able to implement that strategy?

Fifth, can we visit four or five congregations that have designed and implemented a strategy to reach and serve the people who are at the top of our priority list? Can we study what they are doing and adapt their design to our situation? (Examples 2, 3, 7, and 10 represent possibilities for learning from others.) Or will we have to invent and perfect a new model of ministry in order to achieve our goal? (Example 9 is a model that is still a work in progress. In one congregation the leadership team consists of recent new mothers. In another the entire team consists of three grandmothers.)

Sixth, and perhaps most crucial, can we win the support from our members that we will need to make the changes required to implement the strategy? If not, what is our alternative plan?

VI. Growing or Shrinking?

This is a relatively objective line of demarcation for classifying either congregations or denominations. It also is a reasonably consistent indicator to determine which congregations are most likely to be receptive to the changes required to be competitive in the religious marketplace and which are likely to be more resistant to change.

The critical question is what indicator will be used to measure growth or decline? From this traveler's perspective the answer is not baptisms or confirmations. Those tend to be heavily influenced by the age and marital status of the membership. It also is not membership. That often is influenced by whether the congregation has a low threshold at the entrance and a high threshold at the exit or vice versa. This observer strongly recommends that the year-by-year average worship attendance be that indicator. A distant second is whether the total number of new constituents is increasing year after year or decreasing.

The central point is to identify the line of demarcation that separates numerically growing institutions from the numerically declining institutions. This is widely used today in planning for the future of discount stores, institutions of higher education, medical clinics, public high schools, commercial airlines, newspapers, hospitals, financial institutions, museums, supermarkets, health clubs, political parties, cooperatives, parachurch organizations, book publishers, public libraries, dentists, public transit systems, Roman Catholic seminaries, clock repair shops, and long distance trucking companies.

As they plan for their future the list of questions faced by those with an expanding constituency differs greatly from those with a numerically shrinking constituency.

The congregation that averaged 125 at worship a dozen years ago and has watched that number gradually decrease to 58 last year is confronted with a different agenda than the congregation that also averaged 125 at worship a dozen years ago and last year that number was 267.

Another example of that same point is the agendas before the Assemblies of God and The United Methodist Church. In 1952 the Assemblies of God reported 370,000 members in 6,400 congregations. Fifty years later they reported nearly 1.6 million members in 12,133 congregations. One agenda item for those five decades was increasing the number of congregations.

In 1952 the two predecessor denominations of what became The United Methodist Church in 1968 reported a combined total of 9.9 million members in 43,140 congregations. Fifty years later the equivalent numbers were 8.3 million members in 35,102 congregations. One agenda item for those five decades was the merger of two denominations. Another was the merger or dissolution of several thousand congregations.

When the congregational leaders begin the process of designing a ministry plan for the next several years, what drives that process? That question surfaces in all of these categories for classifying congregations. In those churches that have been experiencing a long period of numerical decline, that process should be driven by four questions. First, what have been the outcomes our system has been producing? Second, if those outcomes are undesirable, what are the desirable outcomes? A common response is to reach and serve new constituents. That leads to the third question. What changes in our system must be made to produce those desirable outcomes? Finally, what new or additional resources will be required by that revised system to produce those desired outcomes? That is a simplified explanation for a systems approach to congregational renewal.

V. Large or Small?

What drives the planning process in the congregation averaging fewer than 65 at worship? The most frequent response is lay participation and the search for a consensus. Small Protestant congregations usually tend to perceive themselves to be participatory democracies. When a specific course of action calling for radical change begins to win substantial support, it may be vetoed by one or two families.

What drives the planning process in the congregation that during the past seven years has seen the average worship attendance more than double from 435 to 968? The current senior minister arrived nine years ago and now has seniority over all but one of the paid full-time staff members. One of the three most common answers to that question is the senior minister is the driving force behind the planning process. A second is the program staff team. A third model is the senior minister plus three program staffers plus three widely respected and influential lay volunteers.

Why? In that large and rapidly growing congregation the focus is on evangelism, relevance, and quality, not on making sure every member has a voice in the planning process.

Those three paragraphs introduce the first of what this observer is convinced is one of the five most useful conceptual frameworks for classifying congregations. This system calls for classifying congregations by size using average worship attendance as the yardstick for measuring size. This system divides the estimated 325,000 congregations (exclusive of lay-led house churches) into nine groups. The largest group consists of the 90,000 congregations in American Protestantism averaging 50 or fewer at worship. A second includes another 75,000 averaging 51–75 at worship. A third group includes those averaging 76–100 at worship. The fourth group lumps together the 25,000 averaging 101–125 at worship. Together they account for approximately 70 percent of the congregations under that broad umbrella called American Protestantism.

A fifth and more inclusive group is for the 45,000 averaging 126–200 at worship. The next large group includes the 30,000 averaging 201–350 at worship. When we add the seventh group consisting of 10,000 averaging 351–500 at worship, we can apply the label "midsize" to those 85,000 churches. Together they represent slightly over one-fourth of the congregations in American Protestantism.

The next-to-smallest group consists of the 8,000 "large" churches averaging 501–800 at worship. Finally the broadest range includes the 7,000 "very large churches" averaging more than 800 at worship. A persuasive argument can be made that should be subdivided into two groups, "very large" and "megachurch," but this is not the place to define that line of demarcation! Others have told me they believe that first group of 90,000 churches averaging 50 or fewer at worship should be subdivided into two or three or four groups, but we won't debate that issue here. (WARNING: These are estimates based on the reported attendance of slightly more than one-half of the estimated 325,000 Protestant congregations in America. The methodology probably understates the 50,000 averaging 25 or fewer at worship by at least 5 percent or 2,500, and it may understate the number averaging 800 or more at worship by as many as 10 percent.)

The central value of this nine-compartment category for classifying congregations by size is to affirm differences that are a product of size and complexity. The system for governance that is appropriate for a congregation averaging 85 at worship is not appropriate for the very large church averaging 850 or 1,850 or 3,850 at worship. A long list of other means-to-an-end concerns such as real estate, staffing, financing, the role of lay volunteers, schedules, missions, and the use of modern technology need to be customized by size, as well as by other factors, in the design of a ministry plan for the twenty-first century. That long sentence explains why this traveler has become convinced size is now among the five most useful systems for classifying congregations.

A persuasive argument can be made that size is the most useful system for classifying congregations if the issue is to determine which congregations can both afford and attract a seminary graduate to serve as the full-time resident pastor. Size often is used in defining a congregation's "fair share" of the cost of financing denominational budgets. The projected average worship attendance for ten years from now is also one of the two or three key variables in deciding whether to buy or sell land. How much land will we need to house our ministries a decade down the road? One acre? Three acres? Twenty acres? Two hundred acres?

On the other hand, scores of very small congregations are heavily dependent on modern technology, such as the use of sermons delivered by videotape, while 98 percent of all larger churches still insist the message be delivered in person by a live messenger in that room.

IV. Jerusalem or Athens?

This system can be a useful approach for classifying congregations in terms of their openness to taking advantage of technological advances, which was discussed earlier as system VIII.

Instead of using emotion-laden words such as a conservative or progressive or evangelical or liberal or moderate or orthodox or postmodern in identifying the theological stance of congregations, this approach borrows another line of demarcation.[5] One group of congregations are identified as attracting migrants from Jerusalem (the city of faith) while the second attracts those who were comfortable living in Athens (the city of knowledge). Members of this first group rely almost entirely on Scripture and tradition or creeds in defining the Christian faith while those reared in Athens give more weight to experience and reason than do the folks from Jerusalem. It also should be noted that many of those socialized into the Christian faith as children in Jerusalem have migrated to Athens while others have migrated from Athens to Jerusalem. A significant number of American Christians agree with the Athenians on several issues of faith, but are more comfortable with the Jerusalem perspective on at least a few questions.

CLASSIFYING CONGREGATIONS

THE ISSUE	JERUSALEM	ATHENS
Defining Our Belief System	Scripture, Tradition, Creeds & Sacraments	Experience & Reason
Biblical Theme for Outreach	Matt. 28:18-20	Matt. 25:34-40
Common Sermon References	Second or Third Person	First Person of Trinity
Central Focus of Bible	Salvation	God's Love
Believe John14:6?	Yes!	Yes, but . . .
Scripture Is Marked by:	Certainty!	Ambiguity
Adult Bible Study	"Alpha"	"Living the Questions"
Change the World	Transform Lives of Individuals	Reform Institutions
Affirms the Authority of Denominational Headquarters	No	Maybe
Central Organizing Principle of Ministry Plan	Transformation of Believers into Apostles	Social Justice
Use of Technology	Yes!	That depends
Allies	Coalitions of Jerusalem Congregations	Wide Ecumenical Spectrum
Values	Personal	Communal
Regional Strength	South & West Coast	Northeast & North
Favorite Magazine	*Christianity Today*	*The Christian Century*
Multisite Congregations	Certainly!	No Precedents
Year Congregation Founded?	After 1960	Before 1960
Source of Program Staff in Large Churches	From Within Our Membership	Theological Schools and Midsize Churches

While it is vulnerable to the criticism that it oversimplifies a complex and subjective line of demarcation, the accompanying table represents an attempt to suggest criteria for deciding whether a Christian believer searching for a new church home will choose a congregation led by people from Athens or by those who come from Jerusalem. This system also can be a valuable tool in defining the criteria to be used in selecting the next pastor.

Most of the larger Protestant congregations in America that average more than 350 at worship clearly fit into one of these two groups, but more than a few are largely in one column although they reflect the characteristics of the other column on at least two or three criteria.

That previous system, based on size, may be far more useful in classifying congregations that average fewer than 150 at worship.

III. Maintenance or Viable or Competitive?

From this observer's perspective the second most subjective system described in this chapter and the third most useful for classifying congregations also may be the most rarely used. This approach divides congregations into three groups. The second largest group consists of those smaller congregations that are focused on providing a meaningful ministry to the current membership and on maintaining the status quo. They do not have the resources to compete with all the other Christian congregations for future constituents. Relatively few of their children and youth of today will be members of this congregation in 2035. More members leave because of marriage than "marry in" to these congregations. Deaths may outnumber baptisms. The median age of the members is rising, not dropping. The threshold into full membership usually is low, but few ask permission to cross it. Only a few of these congregations can afford a full-time and fully credentialed resident pastor. The number-one financial asset usually is a parcel of land and a building paid for by earlier generations of members. A tiny proportion, but a growing number, has an endowment fund or a large memorial fund. The income from that fund often is the key in balancing the annual budget. They may not be receiving a direct financial subsidy from their denomination, but many are benefiting from an indirect subsidy. A common way to balance the budget is to defer maintenance on the real estate. The resistance to technological change almost always means the members prefer a sermon delivered in person by a live individual in that room to a much higher quality message delivered via videotape by an exceptionally competent communicator of the gospel. A frequently asked question is, "Who will turn out the lights after the last funeral?" Many of the congregations in this group come from among the 50,000 Protestant churches in America that average 25 or fewer at worship.

In a wonderful book published in 1989 and introduced in chapter 6, Ray Oldenburg suggested most Americans organize their lives around three places. The first place is the home. The second is the place of work. At work people often are identified by what they do or by a title or their professional competence or by the work schedule or by their responsibilities. The third place is represented by those "core settings of informal public life . . . that host the regular, voluntary, informal, and happily anticipated gatherings of individuals beyond the realm of home and work."[6] For tens of millions that third place is where their number-one personal social network gathers regularly. Examples include the bowling league or a street gang or an adult choir or a service club or a neighborhood tavern or a bridge club or a clique at the mall or a coffee shop or an adult Sunday school class or a mutual support group. The crucial distinctive characteristic of a good third place is the participants eagerly look forward to being with their favorite social network in that familiar place. For many of the Protestant churches that are great third places, the people gather at least once a week in a room filled with sacred memories. That, of course, also reinforces a powerful past orientation in planning for a new tomorrow.

One of the disappointments experienced by dozens of denominational leaders has been the merger of two or three of these maintenance-type congregations rarely produces a viable church. Some people prefer the term "marginal" rather than maintenance to describe the 75,000 churches in American Protestantism that fit into this group.

The largest number of congregations can be placed into a second group we will label as "viable." A generous definition of that term is the recent expansion of the old "three-self" concept formulated by Henry Venn and Rufus Anderson during the second half of the nineteenth century. This called for new missions on other continents to be designed to become self-governing, self-financing, and self-propagating. Subsequently Roland Allen and others urged that concept be expanded to include a fourth goal of self-expressing.

That four-self concept can be used to introduce this second group that includes at least 200,000 congregations in American Protestantism. They are largely or completely self-governing, although many are affiliated with a "connectional" denomination that reduces their autonomy. The contributions of current living members do, or at least could, cover all operating expenditures as well as capital outlays. They are not dependent on continuing financial subsidies, either direct or indirect, from a denominational treasury or an endowment fund. They express their own convictions on questions about the interpretation of Scripture or public policy or human sexuality or the use of modern technology or the language to be used in the corporate worship of God.

The congregations in this second group range in size from an average worship attendance of 12 to over 500. Some of the very smallest are economically viable because weekly worship is led by a team of three indigenous members, one of whom is licensed to officiate at the service of Holy Communion. The sermon was prepared and first delivered in another setting by a person who is an excellent communicator of the gospel, videotaped, and delivered in this small church by videotape. Pastoral care is the responsibility of one or two volunteers who have received the appropriate training for that role.

A reasonable guess is one-third of these viable congregations have been experiencing a modest, but not yet threatening decrease in average worship attendance over the past decade, one-half have been more or less on a plateau in size, and perhaps as many as one out of six report their current average worship attendance is higher than it was ten or fifteen years ago. In a relatively few cases the arrival of the current pastor has moved this congregation up out of the maintenance group into the viable classification. In a larger number the arrival of the current pastor was followed either by a drop out of the viable classification into the maintenance group or is producing a reclassification into the smallest of these groups, those designated here as "competitive."

This third group includes an estimated 50,000 Protestant churches in America. Ten of the useful measurable indicators are (1) year after year the number of baptisms or confirmations exceeds the number of member deaths, (2) for the past several years the average worship attendance has been increasing, (3) the median age of the confirmed members has been dropping, (4) the current pastor or senior minister arrived more than seven years ago, (5) at least 10 percent of the total expenditures over the past five years have been allocated to capital improvements including debt service on earlier capital improvements, (6) the ratio of average worship attendance to confirmed membership is over 70 percent, (7) policy-formulation and ministry planning are largely driven by the paid staff, not lay volunteers, (8) the weekend worship schedule gives people a choice of at least two worship experiences, (9) the ratio of church-owned offstreet parking spaces to Sunday morning worship is close to 1 to 2 or at least 1 to 3, and (10) a substantial proportion of the recent newcomers are persons who have migrated here from another church, but not because of a change in that person's place of residence. Most of the congregations in this third group display at least seven of these ten characteristics. The most frequent exception is the current pastor or senior minister arrived more recently than seven years ago.

A common perception by outsiders is most of the competitive congregations are nondenominational and evangelical megachurches founded since 1970. That does reflect one highly visible slice of contemporary reality, but it also oversimplifies the larger picture. Thousands of these competitive churches trace their origins back before 1930 and the vast majority do carry a denominational affiliation.

Five better reasons to explain why these congregations are competitive are (1) they are able to mobilize the resources required to excel in quality, relevance, and choices, (2) they place a high priority on fulfilling the Great Commission (3) most of them have enjoyed the leadership of the same senior minister for at least ten years, (4) the membership has not been polarized by an intradenominational quarrel, and (5) those four assets have enabled them to implement the changes required to be competitive on the religious scene in the twenty-first century.

II. Ministerial Tenure?

Your assignment is to build a list of what you believe to be the 100 outstanding Protestant congregations in America. With one exception you may create your own set of criteria for evaluating candidates for that list. The one required criterion, which is required to be consistent with the theme of this book, is every congregation on your list must be competitive in reaching, attracting, serving, assimilating, nurturing, discipling, and challenging adults born after 1960. Contemporary American Christianity does include scores of congregations that provide rich and meaningful ministries with people born before 1940, but despite the recent advances in medical science, it may not be prudent to build the future with people born before 1925. They can help us maintain continuity with the past, but they should not be asked to design and implement a twenty-year ministry plan.

After you have completed all the traveling required to build that list of 100 outstanding Protestant congregations, what will be the number-one common characteristic? From this sojourner's experiences, one answer will be the continuity in role and relationships. That does not necessarily include continuity in real estate. For most of the history of Christianity in what is now the United States of America, congregations found continuity in the language used in worship, in the ancestry of the members, in a denominational affiliation, in that sacred meeting place, in local traditions, in kinship ties, and in their community image. That was and still is a relevant sentence for thousands of Christian congregations.

Today, all across the American culture, however, continuity is increasingly in interpersonal relationships. The bad description for this is the "cult of personality." The three major television networks, ABC, CBS, and NBC, recently illustrated that as each has replaced the number-one anchorperson for their news telecast with a new personality. Personalities have replaced party names in describing candidates for the presidency of the United States or for the United States Senate. High school and college students choose courses, partly on what is required for graduation, but often on the personality of the teacher.

This traveler's hunch is that after you have compiled your list of those 100 outstanding Protestant congregations in contemporary America, the second most common characteristic will be they have had the benefit of at least one pastorate that lasted more than two decades. That may be the current senior minister or team leader. In perhaps a half dozen or so, that name will be of the senior pastor who left within the past year or two.

While a long pastorate does not automatically open the door to change or produce a congregation that can compete with others for the loyalty of younger generations, it is rare to find a congregation that has been served by a series of two-to-five-year pastorates over the past three or four decades that also is dominated by members born after 1965.

The driving generalization is the larger the size of the congregation and/or the greater the competition among the churches in that community to attract younger generations and/or the larger the number of changes that must be identified, defined, supported, and implemented to reverse years of numerical decline or to move up off a plateau in size and/or the faster the rate of numerical growth and/or the greater the degree of demographic

FROM COOPERATION TO COMPETITION

diversity among the constituents and/or the larger the geographical area to be served by that congregation and/or the greater the degree of theological pluralism in that denominational system and/or the longer that congregation has been in existence and/or the more urgent the need to adapt modern technology, the more valuable is the pastorate of two or three or four decades.

This also becomes a criterion for choosing a successor when the current pastor departs. What is the potential tenure of each candidate? A more important criterion, however, ranks number one in this chapter. This also may be the most common characteristic among the congregations on your list of the 100 outstanding Protestant congregations in America today.

I. A Great Match!

If he was not the best basketball player in the history of American sports, Michael Jordan certainly was one of the five best. He was a great player! It also turned out that Jordan's combination of personality and athletic skills was a perfect match for what the Chicago Bulls needed to win several championships in the National Basketball Association. Jordan earned his recognition as a superstar.

In 1993, shortly after his thirtieth birthday and after he had led the Chicago Bulls to three consecutive national titles, Jordan announced his retirement. He wanted to spend more time with his wife and children. Subsequently he announced he was coming out of retirement to play professional baseball for the Chicago White Sox. Sportswriters speculated Jordan would become the first athlete to earn a place in both the Basketball Hall of Fame and the Baseball Hall of Fame.

Jordan began his new career as an outfielder with the Birmingham Barons in 1994. For the season his batting average was .202, the lowest of any regular player in the Southern League for that year. He struck out in slightly more than 28 percent of the times he went to bat. He returned to professional basketball and in 1995–96 he led the Chicago Bulls to the best single season record in the history of the NBA.

Michael Jordan's combination of athleticism, decades of practice handling a basketball, work ethic, and personality made him a great match with the Chicago Bulls in the 1990s. He was a poor match, however, when he chose to join the Birmingham Barons as an outfielder. A neurologist explained that he knew Jordan would "never make the grade as a major league baseball player . . . That was a bet you could take to the bank."[7] At age thirty-one Jordan's brain was too old to learn the visual-motor skills necessary to hit a major league curveball. This is similar to mastering the skills required to be a competent violinist. The road to achieving that goal begins at age twelve or earlier.

Michael Jordan was a great match when he was drafted to play basketball with the Chicago Bulls. He was a serious mismatch when he was assigned to play the outfield with a minor league baseball team. He did steal 30 bases, but he was caught 18 times.

The parallel is when a minister who was a highly effective pastor with a midsize suburban congregation is invited to become the senior minister at First Church downtown. That may turn out to be a serious mismatch. That does not mean there is anything wrong with that minister. That does not mean there is anything wrong with that church. All it means is the two should not enter into a permanent relationship. A better choice for First Church averaging 650 at worship might be the person who is in the seventh year as the senior associate minister at another downtown church averaging over 800 at worship and located in a similar size and type city.

The first criterion in creating the great matches that enable congregations to adapt to the changes required to be competitive is that combination brought by the pastor of skill set, personality, theological stance, experience, vision, passion, priorities, and leadership. An excellent match, of course, often leads to the second criterion, long tenure.

Before moving on to the next chapter, another comment must be made about this category for classifying congregations. It does not begin with "a good match." Jim Collins articulated a challenging insight when he wrote what have become those six famous words, "Good is the enemy of great." The need in contemporary American Protestantism is for great matches that endure for two or three or four decades!

FROM COOPERATION TO COMPETITION

CHAPTER NINE

What Does "Choice" Mean?

I n recent years the term "choice" has become a code word for describing the position of those who believe pregnant women are entitled to the right of abortion on demand. As explained in chapter 8, for many parents of school-age children, and especially black parents, that word also means parents should have the right to make a tax-funded choice in selecting the school their children will attend.

During the summer of 2002 former President William J. Clinton urged that persons paying into the Social Security fund should be given the choice of designating 1 or 2 percent of the payroll tax they pay into their own personal retirement account. In the 2004 campaign President George W. Bush advocated a similar public policy for reforming Social Security.

One of the big differences between enrolling as a first year student in college or university in 1945 or 1955 or 1965, compared to enrolling in 2005, is that today that first year student will be given greater freedom to choose the subjects to be studied. Another big difference between 1945 or 1955 or 1965 and 2005 is the United States military forces are now composed only of adults who choose to enlist or re-enlist.

During the past few decades the differences among the congregations within each of a dozen large Protestant denominations have become greater than the differences between denominations. One consequence is when the person who has been a member of the same Presbyterian or Methodist or Lutheran or Episcopal or Reformed or United Church of Christ or Baptist congregation for decades moves many miles to a new residence, that churchgoer may switch denominational ties in choosing a new church home. Church shoppers now exercise the right of choice!

Technology-driven changes also have expanded the choices available to churchgoers. A hundred years ago most American churchgoers felt constrained to choose a church within three miles of their place of residence. This coming weekend tens of millions of Americans will drive somewhere between three and forty miles each way in their journey to church. Thirty years ago the pulpit nominating committee might have been forced to choose between two candidates to replace their departed pastor. One clearly was a superb preacher, but ranked low on the scale in terms of skills in interpersonal relationships. The other was a model of the perfect loving shepherd but, at best, a slightly below average preacher.

Which one should they recommend receive the call to fill that vacancy? One attractive option for three out of four Protestant congregations today is to choose the loving shepherd and use videotapes of messages delivered by a half dozen of the nation's most competent preachers. The bonus is that can save the new pastor eight to twelve hours every week that otherwise would be devoted to sermon preparation.

Most Americans born in 1965 have spent four decades being socialized into a culture that offers them a huge range of choices from cereal to beverages to clothing to hobbies to sports to shopping to entertainment to education to transportation to the choice of a job in the labor force to the selection of a spouse to the accessories that come with a cell phone to music to television channels to a pension plan to housing for an aging parent to what happens to the physical remains after death.

One of the most interesting is the choices in housing offered the eighteen-year-old high school graduate enrolling in college or a university.

Perhaps the most highly visible and measurable example of how change drives competition and of how competition influences choices is in commercial air travel. How much will an airline ticket cost to travel between Point A and Point B? The biggest single variable is not the distance, but the choices available to the traveler. If only one airline flies that route, the fare may be triple the fare for twice the distance if that route is served by four or five carriers.

Another example that receives tremendous newspaper coverage every November and December dates back to 1976 when the reserve clause in the contracts for major league baseball players was amended. The old contract that could be renewed annually at the club's option was replaced by a new one that enabled the player to become a free agent after six years. That gave the player a choice in deciding which team to play for in the coming years. The resulting competition for the best players drove up salaries.

Perhaps the most influential example grows out of the fact that millions of today's churchgoers also make a weekly trip to a giant supermarket. The design of that store may include a full-service pharmacy, travel center, bank branch, sushi bar, pie and pastry shop, fresh fruit and salad bar, espresso bar, bagel shop and pizzeria, as well as many aisles of groceries, greeting cards, meats, magazines, beverages, and household supplies. That is consistent with a "good" church including a coffee shop, a bookstore, a wireless room for those using a laptop computer, a nursery, a gymnasium, a soccer field, a weekday prekindergarten program, a prayer room, a skateboard park, and a parish nurse on the staff.

Another is the choices parish pastors are confronted with in scheduling weekend worship in the larger Protestant congregations in America. Fifty years ago the options often were expressed in either-or terms. Should we go to two services or build more space? Should we continue with one service or add an early service to the Sunday morning schedule?

That producer-driven discussion was governed by the calendar, the clock, local traditions, and the assumption that the process was driven by a shortage of resources. As recently as the 1990s the design for the construction of the first meeting place for a new mission or one that was relocating its physical plant was "We need one room for worship, an entrance or 'milling around space' or narthex, one room for fellowship, one room to serve as a kitchen, several classrooms, two or four restrooms, an office area, and corridors." The three big questions were whether that room for fellowship could also serve as the temporary space for worship and whether the acoustics should be tuned for music or for the spoken word.

These are only a few of that rapidly growing number of choices that the American economy now offers people. The question is not whether a plethora of choices is good or bad, but rather will your congregation and/or your denomination respond to the implications of a culture overflowing with choices.

The Consumer-Driven Economy

Is choice the cause or a consequence of the arrival of the consumer-driven economy in America? The best answer is "Yes!" The arrival of this consumer-driven culture is the product of many forces. That includes affluence; egalitarianism; the civil rights movement; the fact that for many Americans instant satisfaction has replaced deferred gratification as they make decisions; feminism; the abolition of the military draft; the twenty-sixth amendment to the United States Constitution adopted in 1971 that granted the right to vote to American citizens age eighteen and over; the shift from a labor intensive to a capital intensive economy in agriculture, retail trade, entertainment, finances, and other facets of the American economy; the increasing proportion of teenagers who graduate from high school; advances in medical science; the redistribution of income; and dozens of other factors. A strong argument could be made that one of the most influential forces to encourage consumerism has been competition.

Lest there be any misunderstanding that the consumer-driven economy is a recent development in the United States, three examples will help correct that error. The big one, of course, is an explanation of why most of the readers of this book were born in the United States. The answer is a few of your ancestors chose to leave the place of their birth and migrate to America because of the attraction of more choices in religion, in employment, in their daily life, and in their personal future. A second is consumerism drove the migration of people who were living in places east of the Ohio River to join the crowds pushing the frontier westward.

One of the most interesting examples was a consequence of compulsory schooling for children. By 1890 a growing number of states were enforcing the law requiring children to attend school. One consequence was a new answer to the question of what children could do in their spare time. The old answer was work or play. Attending school was a new option. They could read. As young boys learned to read, the question arose of what they would read. The first response was the dime novel. These provided reading for boys that was far more exciting than Sunday school leaflets.

Since a central purpose of the common schools was to improve the character of children, a better answer was books that lifted up the importance of self-improvement. Horatio Alger came along to fill that vacuum. His producer-driven theme was the hero represented the boy every parent hoped their child would become. Alger died in 1899. Overlapping his era was Edward Stratemeyer who sold hundreds of millions of inexpensive hardcover books for boys. His success was based on a consumer-driven approach. The hero in his books modeled a boy who represented "what every kid would like to be."

The parallel in American Protestantism today is the competition between two types of congregations. In one the sermon is designed to respond to "the questions I believe church members should be asking." In the other the message is designed in response to "the questions you folks are asking about the Christian faith and how Scripture speaks to those questions." The number of American Christians migrating across that line of demarcation every week is consistent with the point of this chapter. As people believe they have a right to a broader range of choices, one consequence is an increase in competition for future constituents.

Can It Happen Again?

On the other hand this increase in the number of choices clearly is a product of greater competition in a consumer-driven culture. One consequence of greater competition is an expansion in the number and variety of choices. On the American church scene, for example, back in the 1950s, most Protestant congregations offered potential worshipers three choices, (1) come worship God on our turf at the hour we choose on Sunday morning in the way we worship, (2) go elsewhere to church, or (3) stay home.

Today, thanks in part to competition as well as to the expectations brought by younger generations plus a huge expansion in the geographical area covered by "our service area," it is not unusual to find a Protestant church offering people a variety of choices over the weekend at several locations. One example is the weekend worship schedule of a large multisite congregation.

5:00 p.m. Saturday—a traditional service in the sanctuary followed by a meal at 6:15 p.m. at that central location.

6:15 p.m.—Also at that central location, a meal followed by a nontraditional worship service at 7:00 p.m. in the theater followed by an informal sermon feedback discussion in the fellowship hall with people seated at round tables enjoying refreshments while discussing the message delivered in that service. The discussion leader is not the preacher. The goal is an open discussion, not a defensive reaction. The leader is a lay volunteer who is able to replay short passages from that message via videotape.

7:00 p.m.—A worship service ten miles away at the west campus in a church building acquired from a congregation that had disbanded. That service, with 140 worshipers, is led by a team of one staff member plus three lay volunteers. The sermon is delivered via videotape and is the same message that is heard and seen at those other two services.

7:00 p.m.—A worship service held in a vacant store in a strip shopping center eight miles to the south that has been leased for six months as the temporary meeting place for a new worshiping community being organized by this multisite congregation. That service is led by the campus pastor who has been appointed to lead the team to launch this new venture. That campus pastor is assisted by a full-time minister of evangelism and three lay volunteers. About two months ago the attendance plateaued at 325, the capacity of this room. The question is should we add a Sunday morning service—and extend our lease—or look for a larger meeting room?

9:00 a.m. Sunday—A liturgical service in the sanctuary organized around organ music, hymns, the reading of Scripture, prayer, Holy Communion, a homily, and a robed chancel choir.

9:00 a.m. Sunday—A nontraditional service also back at the central location in a room that resembles a theater, except with a flat floor and repeated use of projected visual imagery. It begins with the seven minute "Week in Review in the Life of This Congregation" that includes video clips from a memorial service, three different weekday ministries, two weddings, and a brief report from a missional task force plus announcements of coming events followed by a videotaped call to worship followed by live congregational singing. Subsequent videotaped segments include an introduction to the reading of Scripture, an introduction to the central theme of the message delivered live, the sending out, and the benediction. A twelve-person band plus participatory vocal music provide changes of pace during these seventy-plus minutes.

9:00 a.m.—Two adult Sunday school classes that meet in community rooms in the community center of a retirement village located twenty-two miles east of the home base of this congregation. Both classes are taught by volunteers who reside in this village and helped organize this new worshiping community three years ago. The worship service is held in the larger of these two rooms at 10:30 a.m. and is led by the campus pastor, a chancel choir, and five other volunteers. The message is the same as at the 5:00 p.m. Saturday service back at the home base.

It is delivered by projected visual imagery on one screen. Attendance runs between 115 and 125 on most Sundays of the year.

9:15 a.m.—Three volunteers and a videotape of last night's 5:00 p.m. service arrive to lead worship at this small "adopted" congregation that merged into this missionary church four years ago. The part-time campus pastor is sick today but since this is the same volunteer team that has been appearing for nineteen consecutive weeks, that is not a problem. Five years ago with a part-time lay pastor this congregation was averaging 30–35 at worship. Two years ago the average was 47 and last year it was 53. This Sunday attendance has climbed to 82. Great preaching does attract people!

10:30 a.m.—A traditional worship service in the sanctuary at the home base.

10:30 a.m.—A nontraditional worship service in the fellowship hall with participants seated at round tables. This service is "owned and operated" by approximately two dozen people, one of whom is an ordained minister, three are highly competent musicians, and twenty are lay volunteers in the 16–19 age bracket.

At one end of this spectrum is the producer-driven "This is what we offer. Take it or leave it" style. At the other end of this spectrum is the consumer-driven approach, "We affirm the fact that one format for the corporate worship of God cannot meet everyone's needs. We also affirm the value of offering choices in the day of the week as well as time of the day and in the location of the meeting place." A small but growing number of congregations take this one or two steps farther down the road of multiple choices by scheduling a late Sunday afternoon worship service and/or a Wednesday morning combination worship service-Bible study followed by a meal (most of the participants are mature widows and women living alone) and/or a Thursday evening service for people who leave town late Friday afternoon and return late Sunday.

This spectrum in choices in worship is described to introduce the first big question. Will the day come when this trend will be reversed? That did happen in America in the 1922–45 era. The agricultural depression that began in 1922 was followed by the beginning of an economic decline in 1928 that was followed by the stock market crash in the fall of 1929. That led to the Great Depression of the 1930s. That was followed by World War II. The growth of a consumer-driven economy was halted and the number of choices offered people began to be reduced. The rationing of a variety of goods during the early 1940s was one example of the reduction of choices.

Could it happen again? Could a series of major terrorist attacks on the United States reverse the trends of the past half century? Could a pandemic of avian flu create a scarcity of resources that would reduce choices? Both appear to be a real possibility.

One highly visible cutback in choices in American Christianity can be traced back to the early 1980s, but it did not surface until the early years of the twenty-first century. Those cutbacks were generated by the need to raise the money to pay plaintiffs for charges of pedophilia in Roman Catholic parishes. Those disasters, plus the sharp reduction in the number of parish priests, has produced significant cutbacks in social and educational services as well as in the number of parishes.

Another facet of this first big question concerns the future of several mainline Protestant denominations. Between 1960 and 2000 the population of the United States increased by more than 100 million, or 57 percent, to 282 million. (For comparison purposes the population of the United States back in 1920 was 106 million.) Protestant church attendance on the typical weekend increased by at least 50 percent between 1960 and 2000 and that figure may be closer to 65 percent. Comparisons are difficult because some denominations had not yet begun to report average worship attendance in 1960 while mergers and withdrawals have changed the boundaries of the universe. The United Methodist Church and its two predecessor denominations, for example, did experience a drop of approximately 12 percent in worship attendance between 1960 and 2000 while the Assemblies of God more than doubled their worship attendance. If membership is used to measure changes, the United Church of Christ reported at least a half million fewer members in 2000 than in 1960 while the Southern Baptist Convention reported a 60 percent increase in the baptized membership. The Episcopal Church USA reported a 30 percent decrease in its baptized membership, and the Evangelical Covenant Church of America reported an increase of nearly 70 percent in its membership. That rising tide of population did not lift all the religious ships in the ecclesiastical harbor. One explanation of what it did can be summarized in seven words—greater competition among those ships for passengers.

How Will You Respond?

That long paragraph introduces the second of these two big questions. This continuing cycle of change feeding competition that leads to more changes that generate a higher level of competition that produces more attractive choices for consumers that leads to greater innovation in order to offer consumers more attractive choices that enhances competition appears to be an endless spiral.

How will your congregation or your denominational system respond to this spiraling cycle?

If we look first at congregational life as an institutional expression of the Christian faith in America, we can identify a variety of responses. The most commonly overlooked is in that growing number of house churches with each designed by and for several upper-middle- and upper-class white suburban families. The central organizing principles for many of these house churches include (1) providing a supportive setting to encourage people to share where they are on their personal faith journey with others including their spouses, their close friends, their teenage children, and those who may be a stage or two ahead of them in their own faith journey, (2) caring and mutual support, (3) prayer, (4) the study of Scripture, (5) the worship of God, (6) intimacy, (7) an absence of institutional complexity, (8) a supportive environment for transmitting the Christian faith to their children, (9) an institutional environment that is compatible with designated charitable contributions going directly to an attractive missional cause rather than to institutional overhead, and (10) complete local control over decision making and setting priorities in the allocation of scarce resources such as time, energy, money, and creativity.

Another response is what thousands of small businesses do when they cannot compete in their chosen marketplace. A reasonable guess is in an average year at least 3,000 to 4,000 Protestant churches disappear either by dissolution or by merging into another congregation.

One highly visible response is to grow larger in order to be able to mobilize the resources required to reach and serve younger generations. As the churchgoers born before 1930 disappear from the American church scene, changes are required to continue to be competitive. The resistance to change, however, leads many congregations to choose the road to oblivion.

One common response to the increased competition for future constituents is internal conflict. A related one is that attractive indoor sport called "The Search for Scapegoats."

Another popular, and often more productive option is when the congregation founded in 1882 or 1923 or 1954 as a neighborhood church decides to relocate to a larger site at a better location as it accepts the challenge to become a regional church.

An increasingly common alternative is to specialize in reaching and serving a small but precisely defined slice of the population. Congregation A calls a pastor who is half of a bicultural marriage as one component of a larger strategy to reach and serve adults and their children in a bicultural family. Congregation B focuses its ministry plan on reaching and serving that rapidly growing number of mature Americans who live alone. Congregation C designs a specialized ministry based on the power of music and the research that demonstrates music is the natural channel of communication in the first two or three years of life. The number-one constituency consists of mothers who want to give their new baby a head start in life. Congregation D decides to focus its ministry plan on social justice and serve those who agree the Christian churches should seek to become more persuasive advocates on public policy issues such as peace, poverty, American foreign policy, human sexuality, the criminal justice system, gambling, and education.

Congregation E welcomed a new pastor who brought a contagious entrepreneurial spirit and a conviction that self-imposed ceilings on what can happen do not apply to this church. This congregation was founded in 1881. A farmer donated two acres of land with one acre reserved for a cemetery. A few years later a white frame church building was constructed. In 1911 a basement was dug out under the building. Field stone walls and a concrete floor provided room for a kitchen. The building was renovated as part of the fiftieth anniversary celebration in 1931. A two-story classroom with a first-floor restroom was added in 1958. A few months before his arrival, this new pastor had read Sam Walton's autobiography. He was impressed by Walton's observation that the best place to open a new discount store was in a community that was underserved and where there was little competition. He translated that concept into how it applied to church planning. This open country church was located on what recently had been reclassified from a county road into a state highway. The church site was seven miles south of the small town that included the post office serving this rural area. Twenty miles to the west was the central business district of a city in which the population had doubled from 29,000 in 1950 to 61,000 in 1970 and nearly doubled again to slightly over 118,000 in 1990. The pastor's compelling vision called for transforming this country church into a regional congregation with a special emphasis on reaching and serving the residents to the north and west who wanted to combine a city paycheck with country living. Within two years he had earned the confidence of a dozen allies including the farmer who owned the adjacent land. In 1993 that farmer sold the church three acres of land for $21,000. A year later he gave the church another forty-five acres which were valued at $315,000. The average worship attendance climbed from 47 in 1991, the year this new pastor arrived, to 83 in 1994 to 169 in 1997, the year the first new building was completed, to 485 in 2004, the year after completion of the second building program.

If we shift the focus to responses by denominational systems, we also see a variety of responses. One is denial. "Last year we set an all-time record in contributions received from our affiliated congregations. That suggests we're doing something right, even though our membership is 15 percent lower than it was in 1980."

A second is to expand the number of divisive issues that feed the fires of intradenominational quarreling. That can divert time and energy from confronting the conclusion, "As a denomination, many of our congregations no longer are competitive." A third is to look for scapegoats and conclude the current roster of pastors is the number-one problem.

A fourth option is to buy time by focusing on the courtship that could lead to a merger with another religious body. That was a more popular alternative in the third quarter of the twentieth century that it is today. A fifth has been to "take a more business-like approach and reduce expenditures." A sixth has been to raise more money to fund retirement benefits for the clergy.

A more productive option is to examine the outcomes produced by that denominational system since 1990 and ask, "Are these the outcomes we want our system to produce?" If yes, ask how can we undergird and reinforce the present system so it will continue to produce these desired outcomes? If the answer is no, ask what changes must be made in the system to enable it to produce desirable outcomes?

Examples of relevant outcomes that can be measured with a relatively high degree of objectivity include (1) year-by-year reports on the combined total average worship attendance of all our affiliated congregations, (2) year-by-year reports on the combined total membership, (3) year-by-year statistics for the total number of new members received, (4) year-by-year reports from our affiliated congregations on (a) the number of new members received by intradenominational letters of transfer and (b) the number lost by intradenominational transfers, (5) year-by-year statistics for the annual death rate of our total membership, (6) year-by-year reports on the combined total baptisms, (7) year-by-year reports on the number of (a) new congregations organized, (b) congregations merged with other churches, (c) congregations disbanded, and (d) congregations that terminated their affiliation with our denomination but did not merge or disband, (8) year-by-year reports on the number of affiliated congregations averaging 350 or more at worship, (9) year-by-year reports on the number of congregations averaging 100 or fewer at worship, and (10) year-by-year reports on the combined total number of dollars received by affiliated congregations from contributions of living members.

Most of those measurable outcomes will indicate how changes in the context for ministry and/or the impact of competition and/or the demand for more choices and/or the demand for greater relevance and higher quality are affecting this denomination.

What does choice mean? For most congregations and denominations in American Christianity, it means greater competition for future constituents! To meet that competition may require changes in the design of your plan for ministry in the twenty-first century. A more comfortable choice is to go down the road that leads to obsolescence.

CHAPTER TEN

Who Will Be the Winners?

C ompetition produces winners and losers. The current competition among religious bodies for new generations of constituents is greater than ever before in American church history. The competitors in this free market on the American religious landscape are not playing by the same rule books. A few of these rule books were written back in the 1920s or earlier. Others were written in the 1950s, but several of these have been revised repeatedly to move to the top of the denominational agenda issues that will polarize the current constituency. Many are being written in the early years of the twenty-first century. Several are still in the first draft stage. At least a few have been revised to facilitate the withdrawal of that denomination from a specific city, county, state, or region.

In the year 2030, perhaps sooner, someone will look back and report on the outcomes of this competition during the first quarter of the twenty-first century. That report will identify the winners and losers in this competition for future constituents.

One criterion for predicting that outcome could be who will be most effective in planting new congregations designed to reach, attract, serve, assimilate, nurture, disciple, and challenge the generations born between 1960 and 2010? That turned out to be a useful yardstick for predicting the winners back in the 1865–1915 era. Will history repeat itself?

Another criterion could focus in only on American Protestantism and ask a different question. Which Protestant denominations will include the largest proportion of congregations averaging 3,000 or more at weekend worship? In the year 2030 the response could be, "That was a dumb question! By 2005 it was obvious the answer would be the nondenominational congregations will dominate the large church scene in American Protestantism long before 2025."

An expert on immigration may sharpen the focus more narrowly and predict, "The fastest growing religious body in the United States during the next two or three decades will be one branch of Islam, but at this point in history we cannot identify which expression of Islam that will be."

Those who place a high value on the power of momentum or recent patterns of institutional behavior may predict, "The winners of the past quarter century will be the winners in the first decade of the twenty-first century and the losers of yesterday will be the losers of tomorrow." That has been a useful perspective in predicting the winners and losers in major league baseball in recent years, but does it apply to American Protestantism?

Between 1960 and 2000 two of the big winners on the American church scene were the Assemblies of God and hundreds of nondenominational megachurches. Among the big losers were two dozen annual conferences in what became The United Methodist Church in 1968. Each of those annual conferences reported a decrease of at least 33 percent in confirmed membership over that period of four decades. The denominational mergers among Lutherans and Presbyterians also turned out to be less than universally affirmed winners.

An expert on multiculturalism in America might suggest the fastest growing religious bodies in America between now and 2030 will be those that are most effective in helping to create multicultural congregations averaging more than 3,000 at weekend worship.

That prediction opens the door to discussing the answer that any fan of Peter Drucker will recognize. Drucker states it by reframing the question from, "How can I achieve?" to "What can I contribute?"[1]

The translation of that second question, "What can I contribute?" must be customized to fit a ministry plan for each congregation. The response also must be customized for each religious body. The policy-makers in each regional judicatory, or at the national level, for those with a centralized command and control system of governance, will define both the desired outcome and the process for achieving those desired outcomes. Those policy-makers also will decide whether that customized strategy will be shaped most by listening to (a) one another or (b) the Lord's call to ministry for that particular religious body or (c) the voices of adults and older teenagers who have had their personal spiritual journey enriched by the ministries of congregations affiliated with that denomination[2] or (d) those who are convinced the denominational ministry plan should focus on recreating 1955 with an emphasis on ministries with Americans born before 1930 or (e) leaders who insist the number-one criterion for evaluating the performance of congregations is how they accept and resource denominational goals or (f) the leaders in large and growing congregations that have been effective in reaching and serving Americans born after 1980.

Another perspective is when American churchgoers born after 1960 are asked, "Why did you choose this congregation?" Many reply with a statement that is a personalized paraphrase of Jesus' invitation, "Come to me, all you who labor and are heavy laden, and I will give you rest" (Matthew 11:28 NKJV).

That approach to designing a customized ministry plan may evoke the opposition of those who interpret that simply as another concession to the pressures of consumerism, and therefore it must be resisted.

If a global perspective is preferred, the record of recent years suggests that the expression of the Christian faith called Pentecostalism will be the fastest growing branch of Christianity in the twenty-first century in the United States.

Another perspective that is useful in planning for the future is the self-fulfilling prophecy. To return briefly to the theme of the third chapter, where do you invest your discretionary dollars as you plan ahead to fund the education of your children or to finance your retirement? If you believe the cell phone is a passing fad, you will implement a different investment strategy than if you perceive it to be a symbol of a new era. Likewise, if you believe the fourth great religious revival in American religious history that began in the 1960s came to an end before you read this book, you will design a different ministry plan than if you believe the peak impact of that religious revival lies in the future.

The completely objective and unbiased view of the future of the Christian faith in America does not exist. One expression of a bias is in the next several pages, which describe many of the characteristics of the losers and the winners in this competition. Another expression of a biased view of contemporary reality will be in the reader's responses to these comments.

Before speculating on the characteristics of those religious bodies that probably will be most effective in ministries with the generations of residents of the United States born after 1960, it maybe useful to identify some of the most common characteristics of the losers. Who will be the losers? A reasonable guess is that from the perspective of 2030 the religious bodies that have been least effective in reaching the generations born after 1960 are those that in the first decade of the twenty-first century displayed at least five or six of these dozen characteristics.

Who Will Be the Losers?

The dominant characteristic of one group of losers in both congregational and denominational terms is denial. "Is our system producing too many undesirable and too few desirable outcomes? Yes, but that is not the fault of the system!"

Denial creates a fertile institutional environment for generating a search for scapegoats. Thus denial encourages a defensive diagnosis. "Yes, it's true that our members are growing older in age and fewer in numbers, but that is *not* the problem. Our real problem is our people. If our members would invite their friends, relatives, neighbors, and colleagues at work to come to church with them, all our numbers would be going up, not down. If every member accepted and fulfilled the responsibility to be an evangelist, our churches would be overflowing with people. If all our pastors were better preachers, we would not have any problems. If every one of our denominational officials accepted and fulfilled the call to be a transformational leader, we would not have to be talking about a turnaround strategy. If every one of our members would return even one-half of their tithe to the Lord by way of the treasuries of our congregations and our denominational system, we would not be limited by a shortage of money. If wishes were fishes, only the vegetarians would go away hungry."

One way for your congregation or your denomination to be a loser in this competition is to deny that old system has become dysfunctional. Systems produce the outcomes they are designed to produce! The shortage of money, the decline in worship attendance, the aging and numerical shrinkage in the membership, the scarcity of deeply committed and competent volunteers, the exodus of members to other religious bodies, that large proportion of church shoppers who visit once and never return, that alarming proportion of the teenagers who were confirmed back in 1995 and today have no active relationship with any congregation affiliated with our religious tradition, and the way intradenominational quarreling has taken over the agenda are *not* problems. A more useful diagnosis begins with a brief question. Are those really the symptoms of a dysfunctional system?

One positive response to denial is to flood the system with accurate, relevant, and measurable information that describes contemporary reality. A parallel one is to create a relevant annual audit of performance. A more attractive response is to continue in denial by denouncing "the bean counters." ("Bean counters" has become a nickname for those who focus on outcomes and demand accountability.)

A second and more easily measured characteristic of most of the losers is they will report a decrease in the number of

congregations between 1985 and 2025. That in itself is not especially significant. For example, a healthy denominational system
could produce a decrease of 400 in the number of very small
congregations and an increase of 200 in the number averaging
over 800 at worship. Thousands of congregations disappear
from the American Protestant landscape every year. A better
question asks about what is happening with creation of the new?

What is significant is the reason for that decrease. One explanation is more congregations either merged into another
church or dissolved or withdrew from that larger religious body
than were planted. That suggests more time and energy was
invested in shrinking that number than in increasing it. Given
the zero sum nature of denominational resources that suggests
fewer resources were available to create the new.

Another reason to lift up this indicator is that it is relatively difficult to identify a religious body in American Christianity that
between 1955 and 2005 both (a) increased the total membership
and (b) concurrently reduced the number of congregations.

The most important reason, however, for studying this indicator is that the record to date suggests the Protestant churchgoers in America who were born after 1960 display a clear
preference for pioneering the new and a limited interest in
helping to perpetuate the old. This is most clearly visible
among immigrants who came to America as adults. The planting of new missions and the organizing of new affinity midlevel
judicatories that are not geographically defined, are two ways to
invite younger Americans to help create a new tomorrow.

Third, a common characteristic of those religious bodies that
appear to have decided to discourage the building of relationships with younger generations is to engage in highly visible
and widely publicized intradenominational quarreling. When
recent new members of a congregation are asked, "Why did you
choose this congregation?" a variety of explanations will be
heard. The rarest response, however, is, "We have always
wanted to be part of a larger religious body that places a higher
priority on quarreling than it places on missions, evangelism, or
on transforming believers into disciples."

A fourth common characteristic of the losers of today and tomorrow can be seen in how they articulate their religious beliefs. Those that speak with clarity and certainty about what they believe, preach, and teach clearly are more attractive to the generations born after 1960 than are those who proclaim a message filled with ambiguity.

This is *not* a new pattern! In 1961 the Universalist Church of America came together with the American Unitarian Association to create the Unitarian Universalist Association. That new religious body included approximately 165,000 American members. During the next four decades the membership increased by an average of approximately 1,000 per year. By contrast, the Church of Jesus Christ of Latter-day Saints, a religious body that proclaims its message with certainty, reported a net increase in its membership during that same period that averaged out to 75,000 annually.

That introduces a fifth line of demarcation. Those religious bodies most likely to attract the younger generations are those that place a high value on Scripture, the sacraments, and tradition in proclaiming the Christian faith. Those less likely to attract the younger generations will be giving greater weight to reason and experience.

A sixth characteristic of the losers focuses on the institutional and organizational expressions of the Christian faith. The losers will tend to place a high priority on patching the old wineskins while the winners will be comfortable creating new wineskins to carry the gospel of Jesus Christ to younger generations.

In recent years three of the largest commercial airlines in the United States have discovered that a shrinking number of ticket buyers prefer to travel on an airline that provides generous compensation for the pilots and other employees. One parallel is that tiny number of church shoppers who evaluate congregations on the basis of the compensation and retirement benefits provided to the clergy.

An eighth common characteristic of the losers is they drifted into an institutional culture that conveys the impression to congregational leaders that churches exist to resource the denominational system. Relatively few Protestant churchgoers born in America since 1960 affirm that worldview.

A ninth characteristic of the losers in this competition reflects the post–World War II era in American Protestantism. Denominational mergers and attracting younger generations appear to be incompatible goals. One explanation for that pattern is that denominational mergers require resources that otherwise could be allocated to reaching, attracting, serving, assimilating, nurturing, discipling, challenging, and equipping new generations with the Good News about Jesus Christ. The creation of a new institutional expression of the Christian faith can become a competitor for resources and/or become a polarizing item at the top of the denominational agenda.

Tenth, one significant difference between the generations who were born in the 1920–40 era and those born since 1950 can be summarized in one word. That word is accountability. During the 1940s and 1950s Americans displayed an exceptionally high level of trust in institutions such as the United States armed forces, the public schools, religious organizations, profit-driven corporations, financial institutions, the United States Congress, the office of the President of the United States, and institutions of higher education.

At least a few readers will look back and conclude a new era began with the war in Vietnam in the 1960s and the Watergate scandal a few years later. Others may point to the special commissions appointed to investigate the failure of the Columbia space vehicle and the 9/11 disaster as more recent and constructive demands for accountability. Today Roman Catholic bishops have been called to accountability by the Survivors Network of Those Abused by Priests and the Voice of the Faithful as well as by their National Review Board. Nonprofit hospitals are being challenged by advocates for the poor. The attorneys general of several states are challenging the performance of financial institutions. Alumni are challenging the actions of their university. High school students are demanding greater accountability from the adults who administer those schools. Parents are demanding greater accountability for the policies of the Pentagon. The losers in this competition among American religious bodies for the allegiance of the generations born after 1960 will assume the standards of accountability for policies, practices, priorities, and outcomes that were adequate for the 1950s continue to be adequate in twenty-first-century America.

While many critics dismiss it as another concession to consumerism, an eleventh characteristic of the losers in this competition is they place a low priority on customer service. All across the American economy the winners tend to be the producers of goods and services that have earned a positive reputation for customer service. Listening is one facet of customer service. Proof that the customer's voice has been heard is another facet.

Finally, we come to what several observers of the contemporary American Protestant landscape contend will be the number-one line of demarcation separating the winners from the losers in this competition. It is placed last in this subsection because (1) it is the most divisive, (2) it faces tremendous institutional resistance, (3) too often it is presented in highly attractive but overly simplistic terms, and (4) that attractive language overlooks a crucial point made earlier about the decreasing tolerance for mediocrity. One popular version of this factor is "Empowering the laity." A second is "Affirming the ministry of the laity."

From this observer's perspective a more useful slogan could be, "Challenging, equipping and calling into ministry those gifted laypersons who, in their personal faith journey, have advanced from the role of believers into deeply committed and fully devoted disciples of Jesus Christ." That, of course, is too many words to become a memorable slogan. The key words that must be included are "gifted," "equipping," "advanced," "deeply committed," and "fully devoted disciples." This rejects the notion that any devout Christian can fill any role in the life of a worshiping community or denominational system.

One facet of this affirmation of the role of the laity will be placing a higher value on relevant experience in the labor force and competence than on academic credentials or titles.

One reason this can be described as a safe prediction is this scenario already is being played out in scores of large churches. A better reason is the next two decades will bring a sharp increase in the number of physically healthy, mentally sharp, energetic, gifted, and deeply committed laypersons who, to use Bob Buford's terminology, are ready to move "from success to significance."

The losers in this competition will tend to rely heavily for initiating leadership on the thousands of exceptionally gifted, deeply committed, and unusually competent graduates of theological seminaries. By contrast, the winners will place a greater reliance for that needed initiating leadership on the tens of thousands of exceptionally gifted, deeply committed, and unusually competent laypersons who have experienced success in the secular labor force, have perfected a set of skills that can be utilized in ministry, have mastered the skill to be a lifelong learner, and who are ready to be challenged to enter a new career as an apostle in the ministry of Jesus Christ.

Who Will Be the Winners?

When that book is published in 2030 identifying the winners in this competition, it almost certainly will report that a disproportionately large number of the younger churchgoers in American Protestantism will be found in large regional congregations founded after 1980 and that report an average worship attendance of more than 800. In addition, most of these congregations will have enjoyed the continuity in leadership for at least two decades of the same senior minister or team leader. Many will report a combined average worship attendance of at least 3,000 in at least a dozen worship experiences held at somewhere between three and 300 sites.

Second, instead of affirming mediocre leadership and ministries by describing them as "good," most of these congregations will be acting on the assumption Jim Collins was correct when he declared, "Good is the enemy of great."

One big difference between the first half and the second half of the twentieth century was in the tolerance for mediocrity.

The growing demand for excellence and relevance has drastically lowered the tolerance for mediocrity in recent decades.

That introduces a third characteristic described earlier. The demand for excellence will open the door wider for the laity to share in both designing and in doing ministry.

A fourth characteristic of the congregations and denominations that will qualify as winners in 2025–2030 is both will be guided by a detailed ministry plan. That ministry plan was created and adopted as the product of an earlier decision to choose to "create our own future rather than attempt to perpetuate the past." That ministry plan will include specific, attainable, and measurable outcomes that provide a reference for periodic self-evaluation and corrections as well as for that annual audit of performance.

One process for creating that ministry plan for congregations avoids the temptation to ask the members to vote for or against change. A special Futures Committee is selected and charged with designing at least three and perhaps as many as a dozen scenarios for this congregation that could become reality within a decade. Each scenario builds on one or more assets of contemporary reality. After these scenarios have been sent to every voting member, four congregational meetings are held. The first is a presentation meeting. Each of the various scenarios is described followed by a question and answer period after each presentation.

The second meeting has two purposes. One is to respond to second thoughts and questions. The other purpose is a ballot that enables each person present to rank these scenarios from most preferred to least preferred. A month later at a third congregational meeting the Futures Committee describes any revisions or changes in what have become its three or four preferred scenarios for the future. At the fourth congregational meeting the first ballot is to eliminate the least preferred scenario. A second ballot may be needed to reduce the list to two. If that is not required that second ballot identifies the preferred scenario.

That basic process can be adapted to fit at least one-half of the 240,000 congregations in America averaging 150 or fewer at worship. One common characteristic of the congregations utilizing a process similar to this one is they rank among the smallest 75 percent of all Protestant churches. A second is a preference for following a participatory democracy approach to decision-making. That may be appropriate for the "small church" where the congregational culture declares every member's opinion is as important as the opinion of any other member.

What about the 25 percent that average more than 150 at worship? First, they should act their size. One implication of that is they should not use a participatory democracy approach to governance. They should act like a big institution and use a system of representative government. One reason is the relatively uninformed opinion should not be as influential as the well informed opinion. A congregational meeting may be required for approval of any major change, such as the decision to extend a call to a pastor or to adopt the scenario required for a new era in ministry. The work required to produce that recommended course of action, however, should be the responsibility of a relatively small number of well-informed people. Instead of calling a series of congregational meetings to study and reduce the number of possible scenarios, that responsibility should be delegated to the governing board.

If a congregational vote of approval is required for implementation of the recommended ministry plan, that should offer the members a choice between two alternatives. Here are three examples.

1. Approve as presented or return for further study. Request more details and/or minor revisions.
2. Choose between Plan A and Plan B.
3. Choose between Plan A that requires radical change and Plan B that requires more modest changes.

The choice between perpetuating the status quo and change should not be offered. If that option really existed, this whole process should not have been initiated!

Another common pattern is the larger the size of the congregation and the faster the rate of numerical growth, the greater the influence of the paid program staff in this entire process.

These five paragraphs can be summarized in one sentence. A fourth characteristic of the winners in this competition to attract and serve younger generations is a policy-making process that is supportive of change rather than of attempting to perpetuate the past.

Another way to state that is the pleasure of creating and implementing a vision for a new tomorrow will compensate for the pain of discontinuity with the past and replacing old traditions with new ones.

A fifth characteristic of many, but not all of the congregations classified as winners in 2030 is they either (a) will be affiliated with a denomination that is experiencing numerical growth or (b) will not carry any denominational affiliation or (c) will carry it very lightly. The congregation affiliated with a denominational system that is enjoying success in reaching younger generations can benefit from two facets of that relationship. One is to learn from a system that has been reaching younger generations. The cross fertilization from shared experiences can enrich both partners. Second, winners tend to attract winners. An affiliation with a loser is not the most effective way to attract winners! To be more precise, the numerically growing congregation affiliated with a numerically growing denomination is more likely to be able to attract and welcome newcomers than is the numerically shrinking congregation affiliated with a denomination that is reporting a decrease in members.

From a denominational perspective the winners in this competition also will (a) display a high level of trust in congregational leaders, (b) be organized to encourage horizontal partnerships in ministry rather than a vertical system of control, (c) provide a positive and supportive institutional climate for the emergence of very large regional churches, (d) largely abstain from highly visible and disruptive intradenominational quarrels, and (e) open the doors to enlisting lay specialists for congregational ministries from that growing inventory of adults born in the 1940s and later who are choosing early retirement from the secular labor force in order to fulfill their call to ministry.

Another way to describe this sixth and final characteristic of the winners from a denominational perspective is to view it as a road that has evolved into four paths into the twenty-first century. Each path calls for a different relationship between the denominational system and the affiliated congregations. The first of these four paths calls for a substantial distance between the two as most congregations largely ignore the denominational system. These congregations pay their annual franchise tax but tend to go their own way.

A second path is designed to facilitate what have become increasingly adversarial relationships between congregations and their denomination. One source of conflict is congregational leaders expect the denomination to resource congregations. Many of the denominational leaders, however, expect congregations to support the denominational agenda and to resource denominational causes and agencies with money and volunteers. This path assumes a top-down vertical structure in the denominational organization. Discussions include repeated references to statements in the constitution and/or doctrinal statement of that denomination.

The third path is designed to encourage unilateral withdrawals by congregations as they terminate their denominational affiliation. If that safety valve for withdrawal is not available, another option is schism.

The fourth path is designed to encourage horizontal relationships between denominational agencies and their affiliated congregations. An increasingly common expression of this relationship is the voluntary partnership to create the new. This may be a partnership to plant new missions. It may be a partnership to encourage the emergence of self-identified teaching churches. It may be a partnership to create a new Christian day school for seventh- and eighth- or eighth- and ninth-graders. It may be a partnership to help congregations build a continuing relationship with one or more sister churches on other continents. It may be a partnership to combat the spread of gambling. It may be a partnership to create and administer housing for homeless mothers. It may be a partnership to create destination-type regional congregations that average several thousand in worship every weekend at a 100–300-acre site. It may be a partnership to feed the hungry. It may be a partnership to provide job training and counseling for persons released from prison. It may be a partnership with a large and numerically self-identified multisite missionary church to encourage very small and small churches to seek affiliation with that missionary church. It may be a partnership to help congregations design, create, and administer a weekday early childhood development center. It may be a partnership to help interested congregations make the switch from teaching to learning as they seek to transmit the Christian faith from older believers to younger seekers on a self-identified search for meaning in life.

The winners will choose the fourth of these four paths into the twenty-first century. Most of the losers will be found on the other three paths. The winners will act on the assumption that a continuing and self-perpetuating cycle rests on those three words of change, competition, and choices. Each generates more of the other two.

Who Is Inventing Tomorrow?

Another perspective for predicting the winners and losers shifts the focus from institutions, such as congregations and denominations, to individuals. One answer can be found in the symbolism represented by the cell phone. That explains why that third chapter is included in this book. Who adapted most quickly to the cell phone? People born after 1975. Who resisted that invention and sought to perpetuate the monopoly of the landline telephone? The policymakers in the corporations offering landline telephone service. When were they born?

The guiding generalization is adults in America born after 1950 have dominated the process for inventing the American economy and culture of 2010. Examples include designing and maintaining interactive educational Web sites, creating the modern Protestant megachurch, greatly expanding the role of women in the practice of medicine and the practice of law, the creation of the blogosphere, the research designed to replace the testing of blood as a diagnostic procedure with the testing of saliva, designing effective learning environments for very young children, inventing new uses for projected visual imagery, creating the multisite congregation, transforming the public library from a place to store printed resources into a resource center for self-motivated lifelong learners, the creation of a new generation of Christian music, and replacing Little League baseball fields with skateboard parks.

At this writing the responsibility for perpetuating yesterday is dominated by adults born in 1950 and earlier. The challenge of inventing tomorrow is dominated by people born after 1950, and especially those born in the 1960s and 1970s.

This was written just after 115 cardinals in the Roman Catholic Church, all born before 1955, elected a new pope born in the mid-1920s. Who will lead your congregation, or your denomination, in the competition of the twenty-first century for future constituents? This aging observer's guess is the vast majority of the winners in that competition are now being led by leaders born after 1950.

What's your prediction on the identity of the winners?

Notes

Introduction

1. For a contemporary review of the implications of Sloan's resignation see Robert Beane, "Vision Minus the Visionary," *Christianity Today* (March 2005): 70–72.
2. Lyle E. Schaller, *The Change Agent* (Nashville: Abingdon Press, 1972).
3. The landmark book on the competition among American religious bodies for constituents continues to be Roger Finke and Rodney Stark, *The Churching of America, 1776–1990: Winners and Losers in Our Religious Economy* (New Brunswick, N.J.: Rutgers University Press, 1992). In chapter 6 the authors describe that huge wave of support for greater interchurch cooperation that peaked in the 1920–60 era.
4. Lyle E. Schaller, *The New Context for Ministry: Competing for the Charitable Dollar* (Nashville: Abingdon Press, 2002), pp. 127–333.
5. The historical context for the decision to create a college to train future clergymen is described in J. William T. Youngs, *God's Messengers* (Baltimore: The Johns Hopkins University Press, 1976).
6. Alison Leigh Cowan, "Yale Ending Its Affiliation with a Church in Quest to Be More Welcoming, Yale Is Severing Ties to a Church," *New York Times*, April 12, 2005, A-18.
7. Peter S. Field, *The Crisis of the Standing Order* (Amherst: University of Massachusetts Press, 1998).
8. Robert W. Fogel, *The Fourth Great Awakening and the Future of Egalitarianism* (Chicago: The University of Chicago Press, 2000).
9. Reported in the *Wall Street Journal*, February 28, 2005, page 1, column 6.
10. A more extensive discussion of twenty-one components of a denominational strategy to reverse decades of numerical decline can be found in Lyle E. Schaller, *A Mainline Turnaround* (Nashville: Abingdon Press, 2005), pp. 81–151.

11. Bill Day, *A Study of Growing, Plateaued, and Declining SBC Congregations* (New Orleans, Leavell Center for Evangelism and Church Health, New Orleans Baptist Theological Seminary, 2004). The concluding observation in this survey is "The Southern Baptist Convention is moving from plateau . . . to decline." The four criteria used to evaluate health were membership, baptisms, the member-to-baptism ratio, and at least 25 percent of the membership growth must be from conversions. Day also found while 30 percent of the congregations 10 years old or younger could be described as "Healthy Growing Churches," only 9.2 percent of those founded more than 50 years earlier qualified as healthy. What are the appropriate criteria to be used in evaluating which congregations in your denominations should be defined as "healthy" in the contemporary highly competitive religious climate in American Christianity?

1. The Bar Has Been Raised!

1. These retail prices are from the article by Guy Trebay, "Who Pays $600 for Seams?" *The New York Times*, April 21, 2005, Section G, pages 1 and 6.
2. The decline in the influence of national ancestry in how Americans identified themselves is described in Will Herberg, *Protestant, Catholic, Jew* (Garden City, N.Y.: Doubleday & Co., Inc., 1955).
3. An easily accessible description of that emphasis on interchurch cooperation is Rodney Finke and Rodney Stark, *The Churching of America, 1776–1990* (New Brunswick, N.J.: Rutgers University Press, 1992), chapter 6. See also James H. Madison, "Reformers and the Rural Church, 1900–1950" in *The Journal of American History* 73 (1998): 645–68. An appraisal of comity and its limitations can be found in Lyle E. Schaller, *Planning for Protestantism in Urban America* (Nashville: Abingdon Press, 1965), pp. 96–120. One contemporary expression of intercongregational cooperation involving very small congregations and large churches is described in Lyle E. Schaller, *Small Congregation, Big Potential* (Nashville: Abingdon Press, 2003), pp. 79–103.
4. For one perspective on why so many teenagers are bored, see Lyle E. Schaller, *The Evolution of the American Public High School* (Nashville: Abingdon Press, 2000).

5. For a brief overview of this erosion of congregational support for denominational budgets see Kathryn Sime, "Crisis or Opportunity?" *The Lutheran* (March 2004): 40–41.
6. James Turner, *Without God, Without Creed: The Origins of Unbelief in America* (Baltimore: The Johns Hopkins University Press, 1985).
7. That is a dominant theme of Leon Howell, *United Methodism @ Risk: A Wake-Up Call* (Kingston, N.Y.: Information Project for United Methodists, 2003). This observer's response was that The United Methodist Church is deeply divided over control, biblical interpretation, and a dozen other issues. Lyle E. Schaller, *The Ice Cube Is Melting* (Nashville: Abingdon Press, 2004).

2. What Do the New Rule Books Say?

1. Nick Morgan, "The Kinesthetic Speaker: Putting Action into Words," *Harvard Business Review* (April 2001): 113–120.
2. This "value added" option for small congregations is described in Lyle E. Schaller, *Small Congregation, Big Potential* (Nashville: Abingdon Press, 2003), chapters 6 and 7.

4. What Are the Consequences of Competition?

1. Jim Collins, *Good to Great* (New York: Harper Business, 2001).
2. Lyle E. Schaller, *The Evolution of the American Public High School* (Nashville: Abingdon Press, 2000).
3. Thomas J. Peters and Robert H. Waterman, Jr. *In Search of Excellence* (New York: Harper & Row, 1982).
4. This summary of Sam Walton's career is drawn largely from Bob Ortega, *In Sam We Trust* (New York: Times Books, 1998).
5. For a more comprehensive discussion of alternative scenarios for small and midsized congregations, see Lyle E. Schaller, *The Small Membership Church* (Nashville: Abingdon Press, 1994), pp. 89–131.
6. An excellent resource for moving an institution from denial to reality is Larry Bossidy & Ram Charan, *Confronting Reality* (New York: Crown Business, 2004).
7. Howard E. McCurdy, *Faster, Better, Cheaper* (Baltimore: The Johns Hopkins University Press, 2001).
8. The annual audit of performance with a strong emphasis on outcomes is discussed in greater detail in Lyle E. Schaller in *A Mainline Turnaround* (Nashville: Abingdon Press, 2005), pp. 39–50.

9. Marvin T. Judy, *The Larger Parish and Group Ministry* (Nashville: Abingdon Press, 1959). Judy was one of the pioneers in promoting cooperative ministries in rural America in the 1950s.

10. Robert William Fogel, *The Fourth Great Awakening & the Future of Egalitarianism* (Chicago: University of Chicago Press, 2000). An exceptional book on this subject is Aaron Wildavsky, *The Rise of Radical Egalitarianism* (Washington, D.C.: The American University Press, 1991). Another is Robert H. Wiebe, *Self Rule* (Chicago: University of Chicago Press, 1995), pp. 181–286. A provocative analysis is Christopher Lasch, *The Revolt of the Elites and the Betrayal of Democracy* (New York: W. W. Norton & Company, 1995).

11. A thoughtful critique of one early version of participatory democracy is Daniel P. Moynihan, *Maximum Feasible Misunderstanding* (New York: The Free Press, 1969).

12. William W. Cutler III, *Parents and Schools: The 150-Year Struggle for Control in American Education* (Chicago: University of Chicago Press, 2000). Michael E. Manley-Casimer, editor, *Family Choice in Schooling* (Lexington, Maine: D. C. Heath and Company, 1982). Gary Burtless and Christopher Jencks, "American Inequality and Its Consequences" in Henry J. Aaron, et al., editors, *Agenda for the Nation* (Washington, D.C.: Brookings Institution Press, 2003), pp. 61–108.

13. For a review of this Board's report see Joe Feuerherd's review in the *National Catholic Reporter* (March 12, 2004): 3–6.

14. Leon Howell, *United Methodism @ Risk* (Kingston, N.Y.: Information Project for United Methodists, 2003).

15. Lyle E. Schaller, *The Ice Cube Is Melting* (Nashville: Abingdon Press, 2004).

16. The best analysis of the popularity of this game that this observer has read is William Sachs and Thomas Holland, *Restoring the Ties That Bind: The Grassroots Transformation of the Episcopal Church* (New York: Church Publishing Incorporated, 2003).

17. For one explanation of why preachers no longer read sermons while standing in the pulpit see Nick Morgan, "The Kinesthetic Speaker: Putting Action into Words," *Harvard Business Review* (April 2001): 113–120.

18. For a longer discussion on various expressions of the multisite missionary church see Lyle E. Schaller, *Small Congregation, Big Potential* (Nashville: Abingdon Press, 2003), pp. 79–110 and J. Timothy Ahlen and J. V. Thomas, *One Church, Many Congregations: The Key Church Strategy* (Nashville: Abingdon Press, 1999).

19. Howell Raines, "My Times," *The Atlantic Monthly* (May 2004): 49.
20. The impact of matching the appropriate leadership with the large urban institution is a central theme of Adam Gopnick, "Under One Roof: The Death and Life of the New York Department Store," *The New Yorker* (Sept. 22, 2003): 92–103.
21. The perspective of one bankruptcy court judge is, "Bankruptcy and the Catholic Church," *America* (Nov. 29, 2004): 18–20.
22. A provocative dissent to *The 9/11 Commission Report* was carried by the *New York Review of Books* (Aug. 29, 2004): 9–11. The use of imagination in planning for the future is illustrated by Richard A. Clarke, "Ten Years Later," *The Atlantic Monthly* (January/February 2005): 61–77. The theme is looking back from September 11, 2011 to describe the terrorist attacks in the pre–2011 years.
23. A provocative review and interpretation of the report on the Columbia disaster is William Langewiesche, "Columbia's Last Flight," *The Atlantic Monthly* (November 2003): 58–87.
24. Howell Raines, "My Times," *The Atlantic Monthly* (May 2004). A sequel to Raines's story is Todd Gitlin, "Media: It Was a Very Bad Year," *The American Prospect* (July 2004): 31–34.
25. Peter F. Drucker, "What Makes an Effective Executive," *Harvard Business Review* (June 2004): 58–62.

5. What Do You Count?

1. Dan Hurley, "Divorce Rate: It's Not as High as You Think," *New York Times* (April 19, 2005): F-7.

6. What Is a Stability Zone?

1. Bill Day, *A Study of Growing, Plateaued, and Declining SBC Congregations* (New Orleans, Leavell Center for Evangelism and Church Health, New Orleans Baptist Theological Seminary, 2004).
2. These are among the twenty-one components of a strategy to renew the numerical decline of a denomination described in Lyle E. Schaller, *A Mainline Turnaround* (Nashville: Abingdon Press, 2005), pp. 81–151.
3. Alvin Toffler, *Future Shock* (New York: Random House, 1970), 324–29.
4. Ray Oldenburg, *The Great Good Place* (New York: Paragon House, 1989).

5. For a longer discussion of the road to multiculturalism from a denominational perspective, see Lyle E. Schaller, *What Have We Learned?* (Nashville: Abingdon Press, 2001), pp. 197–213.

8. What Are Useful Categories?

1. An excellent introduction to the history and value of classification systems is Geoffrey C. Bowkes and Susan Leigh Star, *Sorting Things Out: Classification and Its Consequences* (Cambridge: Mass.: The MIT Press, 1999).
2. Lowell C. Rose and Alec M. Gallup, "The 36th Annual Phi Delta Kappa/Gallup Poll of the Public's Attitudes Toward the Public Schools," *Phi Delta Kappan* (September 2004): 41–56.
3. Will Herberg, *Protestant, Catholic, Jew* (Garden City, N.Y.: Doubleday & Company, 1955).
4. Lyle E. Schaller, *From Geography to Affinity* (Nashville: Abingdon Press, 2003).
5. This line of demarcation was described by James Nuechterlein, "Athens and Jerusalem in Indiana," *The American Scholar* (Summer 1988): 353–68.
6. Ray Oldenburg, *The Great Good Place* (New York: Paragon House, 1989).
7. Harold L. Klawans, *Why Michael Couldn't Hit* (New York: W. H. Freeman and Company, 1996), pp. 1–8, 25, 37.

10. Who Will Be the Winners?

1. Two excellent brief introductions to Drucker's accumulated wisdom are Peter F. Drucker, "What Makes an Effective Executive," *Harvard Business Review* (June 2004): 58–63 and the foreword by Jim Collins to Peter F. Drucker, *The Daily Drucker* (New York: Harper Business, 2004), pp. vii–x.
2. One revealing research project on this source of information is William Sachs and Thomas Holland, *Restoring the Ties That Bind* (New York: Church Publishing Incorporated, 2003).